Law and Power
in International Relations

STUDIES IN INTERNATIONAL POLITICS
(Editor: F. S. Northedge)

Other books in the series

The Foreign Policies of the Powers
edited by F. S. Northedge

The Use of Force in International Relations
edited by F. S. Northedge

Deterrence and Persuasion
French Nuclear Armament in the context of national
policy 1945–1969
by Wolf Mendl

The United Nations System
An Analysis
by Mahdi Elmandjra

International Theory and European Integration
by Charles Pentland

Law and Power
in International Relations

JAMES FAWCETT

faber and faber

© 1982 by James Fawcett

British Library Cataloguing in Publication Data

Fawcett, James
Law and power in international relations.
1. International law   II. International relations
I. Title
341   JX1395

ISBN 0–571–10537–8

Contents

INTRODUCTORY   *page* 9
    The elements of political community   10
    The origin and discontinuity of legal order   18

1 INTERNATIONAL CONTEXTS OF LAW AND
    POWER   21
    The units and operators   21
    Some objectives of policy   26
    The place of law in international society   35

2 POWER FRONTIERS   48
    Frontiers of China   48
    Power-frontier confrontations: Berlin (1948–58) and
        Cuba (1962)   63
    Control of intervention: Suez (1956) and Afghanistan
        (1980)   70

3 ECONOMIC POWER   80
    Protection of investment   80
    The GATT   85

4 HUMAN RIGHTS   91
    Rhodesia (1965–)   92

5 NON-INTERVENTION   111

6 AN OPINION   117

    NOTES   120

    ANNEX   127

Introductory

The approach of the practitioner to international relations, and to the roles of law and power in them, will necessarily differ from that of the observer. Typical practitioners are ministers, diplomats and their legal advisers; typical observers are political scientists and jurists. But they are not of course wholly separable. The prime task of the minister is the formation and execution of policy, and of the political scientist the construction of theories or models of international relations. Again the legal adviser is concerned, often in an adversary role, with how far the law can support or may hinder a particular policy or course of action, while the jurist is concerned with the general characteristics and function of law. But each can be influenced or guided by the other.

In what, then, must be a work of observation of law and power in international relations, it has still to be decided whether it will propound one or more theories or will offer descriptions using certain working concepts, and so follow rather the approach of the practitioner.

Whether there can be a science of international relations, and whether the construction of theories of international relations is possible, are questions which are much debated. A scientific theory might be expected to present an identification of some related facts, a systematic explanation of these facts, and a basis of prediction from them of certain future events. It is difficult to see how a theory of law and power in international relations could be constructed which would meet these requirements. In the first place, though all acts and decisions in international relations are reducible in the end to those of individuals, only aggregate behaviour can be adequately studied. So Morton Kaplan has observed that: 'Nations are built of hundreds of thousands of crosscutting social roles', but 'Structural features chosen to classify national actors are quite gross, and therefore are not sufficient for any analysis aspiring to high predictive power.' Secondly, the time-factor is generally large so that not only are the identifiable facts increasingly variable, but unpredictable events occur to disturb the process of explanation, and it can hardly then be systematic.

The construction of *models* of international behaviour may be more realistic in so far as they are adapted to the identifiable facts and are not predetermined by the assumptions of any one system. Gaming models are of this kind and may be themselves ways of testing models. But they too have their limitations. Gaming models tend to reduce all international relations to forms of competition or conflict; and zero-sum notions are, as often applied to international conflicts, no longer adequate. International conflicts have been described as 'n-person non-zero-sum games in which the pay-off consists for the most part in staying indefinitely in the game'. So, while a zero-sum game is one in which one player wins (I) and the other loses ($-$I), the purpose of a player of a non-zero-sum game is not to defeat the other players but to gain as much ground or profit against them as possible. So war, up to at least the beginning of the twentieth century, was not designed to *eliminate* the antagonist, and there were consequently 'laws of war', a concept not so paradoxical as it now appears. War had a legal status, beginning with a declaration and ending with an armistice to terminate the fighting, and a peace treaty to secure a final settlement. Further, it was a conflict between states and so confined in law to the conduct of hostilities by their agents, and recognized armed forces. Non-combatants were entitled to respect and protection; neutral states and their citizens had a recognized status; and there were rules for the protection of private property during military campaigns. But in this century the technological advance in weaponry has come to the point where there are no longer only two models of international conflict—a zero-sum game and non-zero-sum game—but a second kind of non-zero-sum game in which both sides can lose—hardly a game.

This work will then for these reasons not offer theories or models, but rather a description of how law and power work with and against each other in international relations.

The elements of political community

Aristotle, in one of his characteristic telegrams, tells us that ἄνθρωπος ἐστὶ πολιτικὸν ζῷον. The equally terse translation, that man is a political animal, would have for each word false overtones; and it would be closer to the complex thought to express it by saying that it is the habit of human beings to live in communities, of which the Greek πόλις or city-state was for Aristotle a prime example. From this we can derive some working concepts.

A human community involves some combination of wills, expressed both in free and organized behaviour; and so the notion of community differs from that of society in that it is in the broad sense political, expressing this combination. Metaphorically speaking we might compare human communities with the physical associations of matter. So human beings could be seen as the elementary particles, combined in small or large, tight or loose atomic and molecular structures, ranging from the family to the UN. As in atomic and molecular structures there are physical forces that bind the particles together and forces that may repel them from each other; further, these forces may be strong or weak and are limited in the distances over which they operate. But the weakest of the physical forces—that of gravity—has the distinction of operating without the limit of distance imposed on the others, and here there is strong analogy with law: so law is a weaker bond than love, loyalty or moral compulsion, and is not always, as a source of civic duty, able to contain the forces of competition, dissent or aggression within a particular community. But there are general principles of law recognized as operating, with varying strength, around the world. Again, individuals and groups in human communities are, like physical matter, not only arranged in hierarchies of increasingly complex structures, but they exhibit strong inertial forces in the forms of traditional attitudes and beliefs and habitual ways of doing things.

Law and power are, then, forces, which are not only variable from community to community and differ from each other greatly in strength, but are still essential to the organization and function of a community. It is then a mistake to polarize them. We can think of extremes where power is total or where law is total: for example, at the centre of armed conflict or in an absolute dictatorship, law is virtually excluded; again, in a monastic order, humility and obedience may subject a member wholly to rules. But in general the structure and stability of a community depend upon both law and power. If it were possible to quantify them, they could be placed in a system of Cartesian coordinates and a graph made indicating the relations between them.

We have then to make some inquiry into the nature of political

11

community in order to see whether or how far the notion of community can be applied to international relations.

Prime elements in a national community may be seen as a will to associate, a will to dissociate, a territorial base, and the recognition and distribution of power; though the description of a community in these terms does not necessarily serve by itself to explain the origin of a given community or how or why it holds together.

For an established community *the will to associate* is described in certain axioms or fictions: for example, that the will or tendency to form communities is naturally inherent in human beings, or is embodied in a kind of contract between them, concluded by way of choice or of necessity. Some brief illustrations may be given.

Suarez (1548–1617) regarded the family or *societas domestica* and the community or *societas civilis* as forms of association created *ex vi rationis naturalis*, other associations or *collegia* being established by acts of positive law. These two dominant forms of human association were derived then from the nature of man, as a vehicle of natural reason or order, and beyond that enquiry need not go. But he expressly stopped short of recognizing the association of nations or *societas gentium* as a community, invested with an *imperium mundi* or kind of internationalized sovereignty: for although this *societas* reflects in part a unity of the human race, it is *quasi-politica et moralis*.

This notion of natural association can be found in the evolution of at least some communities. So Bülck[1] describes how clans represent 'continual segmentation' in the face of 'complementary opposition', and may amalgamate—the Roman *curia* was composed of *gentes*. The clan is a kind of extended *societas domestica*; in Greek culture θέμις, or custom accepted as tules,[2] formed the legal order of the clan. Bülck states that tribes are the largest communities, with a legal order, in primitive cultures, depending in part on enacted rules. A further stage is the formation of tribal alliances, where we have an analogy in international relations.

The notion of social contract comes perhaps closer to an explanation of the origin or basis of political community, but rarely corresponds to any human event leading to the formation of such a community, though the adoption of the Constitution (1937) by 'the people' in Ireland outside any legal continuity with United Kingdom legislation—the principle of autochthony—may be an actual social contract. But generally the social contract is a logical presupposition of legal order.

So for Kant the concept of the autonomous individual is logically prior to that of community, the individual surrendering his freedom to receive it again as a member of the community; and Locke had also seen the social contract as being positively affirmed by any citizen who, on coming to the age of majority, opts to remain in the community. Similarly Grotius described the law of nations as *ius gentium voluntarium inter civitates*. Is then the autonomy of the individual, or the sovereignty of the state, an absolute freedom, qualified only by consent? Hobbes, considering that, far from an inherent tendency or readiness of individuals to associate together, there was in the state of nature a perpetual war of all against all, thought that this war could be ended only by voluntary submission and obedience to a common superior. To achieve this then the social contract was both a *pactum unionis* and at the same time an agreement for subordination or *pactum subjectionis*.

Sartre stays with the absolute freedom of the individual,[3] but with a pessimism[4] provoked by the bitter experiences of the occupation of France: '... man is nothing else but what he proposes; he exists only in so far as he realizes himself, and is therefore nothing else but the sum of his actions ... man *is* freedom.' In the confrontation then with other individuals as objects, there is 'the revelation of the other as a freedom, which confirms mine, which cannot think or will without doing so either for or against me'. But in this permanent conflict of freedoms, the individual preserves an absolute freedom of choice either to submit to the decisions of others, which may restrain his actions, or to commit suicide. This almost pathological individualism of Sartre has an analogy in the absolute sovereignty of States, seen as international units. But the ultimate choice offered by Sartre, subjection to order or suicide, reveals two forces at work, the need to survive and what Freud described as the instinct for death or destruction. It is possible then that the degree of subjection to order is a function of the need to survive for the individual and then for the community itself. So a social contract can be seen as largely voluntary, with a limited subjection to order in the early life of a community, where rules will extend little beyond family life, land-holding and the getting and distribution of food. But as the community evolves into greater complexity and the interdependence of its members increases in many ways, subjection to order becomes necessary not only for survival but for the realization of emerging social objectives, and so rules are steadily extended.

The international community is still at an early stage of its evolution, having not yet advanced far beyond tribal alliances. But the interdependence of nations has grown with increasing rapidity in this century, and the subjection of States to some international order is visibly moving from bare consent to necessity; and perhaps the ultimate choice of Sartre is already presented by the emergence of nuclear weapons. Is there even for developed communities a Freudian instinct for death or destruction expressed in their obsession with them?

The size of a community, in regard to the number of its members, is of critical importance. When a community has passed a certain size there must be, given the practical limits to total participation of individuals in all communal decisions, a transfer of at least some of these decisions to certain persons or groups, to the common superior of Hobbes. So Rousseau observed that: 'au lieu de la personne particulière de chaque contractant, cet acte d'association produit un corps moral et collectif lequel reçoit de cette même action son unité, sa vie et sa volonté.'

The will and authority of such a community is often said to come from the people. So in the Federal Convention in 1787: 'We the people of the United States do ordain and establish this Constitution for the United States of America', and the words are echoed in the opening of the UN Charter: 'We, the peoples of the United Nations ... have resolved to combine our efforts to accomplish' the stated aims. But 'the people' as the source of power and authority in a political community, is, save perhaps in the kind of micro-state of about five thousand people envisaged by Plato, in part a fiction like the social contract itself. Walter Lippmann has remarked that the participants in the Federal Convention in 1787 were less than 5 per cent of 'the people' which itself politically excluded women and slaves; and in the establishment of a constitution, 'the people' may be variously the voters in a national referendum, or the representatives in a constituent assembly, or the members of an established legislature. The sovereignty of the United Kingdom Parliament, and in the last resort of the Queen and House of Commons, appears to embody the last-named notion of 'the people' in that the elected members are conventionally representatives and not delegates of 'the people'. That 'the will of the people' is a political fiction is further demonstrated by the fact that, in at least half the member countries in the UN, there is either a one-party system or military rule.

Gierke distinguished the notions of representation of the people, and the transfer or delegation of authority to a 'sovereign', by postulating two contracts: a contract of association (*Gesellschafts-vertrag*) by which the political community is established, and a contract between the community itself and specific agents or organs of government, by which public authority is delegated to them (*Herrschaftsvertrag*).

The will to dissociate, expressed in varying forms of dissent, is accommodated in a political community by the practice of majority rule, which rests on a postulate of equity, that goods or power must be distributed among the population according to numbers. The will to dissociate may range from dissent over particular policies through expression of separate interests to alienation or demands for self-determination. James Madison said:[5] 'By a faction I understand a number of citizens, whether amounting to majority or minority of the whole, who are united and activated by some common impulse of passion, or of interest, adverse to the rights of other citizens, or the permanent and aggregate interests of the community.'

Alienation may find its expression in, for example, anarchism or, in a more limited way, in pacifism as a moral refusal to serve what the community regards as a basic need, its physical defence. Again society may be regarded not as a community, but as confrontation. So Marx saw the capitalist system as one in which the producers are transformed into wage-workers, and the 'relations of production' increase their number, while the number of owner-capitalists is reduced by competition.[6] The 'fundamental contradictions' are worked out in the class-struggle, in which the State is the legal superstructure, Parliament being the 'executive committee of the bourgeoisie', and a main instrument of oppression. The will to dissociate has been translated into contemporary doctrines such as that all government and actions of government are forms of violence, and must be opposed by violence;[7] or that international investment and trading practices are in their nature means of oppression and exploitation of the poor countries by the rich; or that there is a new and critical polarity between countryside and city. The latter two ideas were joined by Lin Piao when he observed in 1965 that: 'The countryside and the countryside alone, can provide the revolutionary bases from which the revolution can go forward to final victory.' Transferring this to the international plane, he described North America and Western Europe as 'the cities of the world', and Asia, Africa and Latin America, as 'the countryside of the world', and he called for the encirclement of the cities by the countryside.

An expression of a will to dissociate, which can have impacts on international relations, is the demand for self-determination by the peoples of dependent territories. The principle has been much invoked since 1945 and self-determination has even been described as a legal right. The UN Charter, in Article 1(2) setting out its purposes, and again in Article 55, calls for 'the principle of equal rights and self-determination of peoples'. The Universal Declaration of Human Rights does not speak directly of self-determination, but the subsequent General Assembly Resolution 637–VII declared that: 'the right of peoples and nations to self-determination is a prerequisite to the full enjoyment of all fundamental human rights'; and it called for information, to be provided under Article 73c of the Charter, on the exercise of the right to self-determination by the peoples of non-self-governing territories and in particular on: 'their political progress and the measures taken to develop their capacity for self-administration, to satisfy their political aspirations, and to promote the progressive development of their free political institutions'. The right to self-determination was reasserted in General Assembly Resolution 1188–XII, and finally stated without qualification in the celebrated Declaration on the Granting of Independence to Colonial Countries and Peoples: Resolution 1514–XV, the second paragraph of which says: 'All peoples have the right to self-determination; by virtue of that right they freely determine their political status and freely pursue their economic, social and cultural development.' This paragraph now constitutes Article 1(1) of each of the UN Covenants on human rights;[8] and, since it is not expressly excluded, it appears that the right to self-determination may be invoked on behalf of a 'people' by a State before the UN Human Rights Committee established under Part IV of the Civil and Political Rights Covenant.

Whether this right to self-determination can properly be described as a legal right is questionable, and the answers must depend on definitions of law. If, for example, a right can be characterized as legal if it is identifiable in terms of its holder and its content and is enforceable by some recognized and available process, then the right to self-determination, as declared in the international instruments, does not appear to meet either of these criteria. In the first place, the term 'peoples' is too indefinite, since it is uncertain what and how many common elements a group must have to rank as a people entitled to self-determination. Will a common religious belief be by itself sufficient? Does a distinct group, with its own language, religion and culture, cease to be a 'people' by integration in an independent state? Are the inhabitants of Quebec, Brittany, Gibraltar

16

or 'Kurdistan', 'peoples' entitled to self-determination, or only those of Gibraltar, being still a colony? Secondly, if Article 1(1) of the Civil and Political Rights Covenants is said to establish self-determination as a legal right, it has to be asked how it is to be enforced; neither Articles 41 and 42 of the Covenant nor the optional protocol offer more than a process of conciliation of demands by a people for self-determination, opposed by the State under whose jurisdiction they live.

Finally, a *territorial base* is essential for a political community, for this provides its elemental living space; a realm of land, air and water with all their resources. It is also in law that defined and recognized area, in which the power of the community can be exclusively exercised. It is said that human beings have, by primeval inheritance, a territorial imperative which determines many of their social conditions and actions; and it is certain that conflicts over territory and its boundaries, and the inward and outward pressures along power frontiers as boundaries of a higher order, are prime elements in international relations.

What is power? In its primitive form power is the ability to induce others to act, or not to act, by the use of physical force or threat of its use. In a political community it is the ability to make decisions and choices on behalf of or affecting others, which they will or must accept largely for two reasons. First, in a community above a minimal size and not based on anarchist principles, it is impossible for all the needs of each member to be secured by personal decision or choice; many decisions and choices must then be delegated. Secondly, physical force, actual, potential or symbolic, remains a constituent of power. In a political community, then, certain persons, acting alone or in combination, obtain or are accorded the power to formulate and choose national policies, to determine the use of national resources, to prescribe rules and standards in many fields, and to control and use the armed forces and police as instruments of force. In most forms of ordered government, power is distributed between legislature, executive and judiciary, according to varying patterns, determined by the extent and kind of power accorded to each, and the degree of subordination of any one power to another. Even under military rule, where the armed forces absorb some or all the functions of the other units, there may be still some distribution of power in fact for: 'Armies themselves reflect many of the cross-currents of ethnic, national, social and political divisions within the broader community; and once the army . . . takes over the control of govern-

17

ment, it soaks up conflicts like a sponge.'[9] In most contemporary political communities there is a distribution of power which defeats any attempt to locate sovereignty or supreme power in any one person or even a single body of persons. The exercise of power, as collective or public authority, in a community is then assigned to a number of persons and groups by delegation or representation.[10] So the 'State' is itself a fiction, and all propositions containing the term must be ultimately reduced to statements about the acts, competence to act, or intentions of, particular persons or bodies of persons.[11]

However, the term 'nation-state' is a convenient shorthand for the political communities which are recognized as principal units of international relations. By way of summary of what has been said above, nation-states may be said to be communities in which there is a system of laws and bodies with law-making powers; an executive capable of administering the national territory with means available to control law-breaking and violence; and courts able to settle disputes according to law and enforce the criminal law. The whole constitutes a legal order.

In certain legal concepts of international relations such nation-states have been traditionally described as sovereign and independent. Sovereignty is the internal and domestic power, just described, and its legal area is the domestic jurisdiction of the State. Independence is an aspect of the State, marking its freedom to manage its own affairs without outside interference or intervention, and to conduct its relations with other States as an equal. These concepts are expressed in the UN Charter, Article 2, which states that the Organization is founded on the principle of sovereign equality of its members: Article 2(2); and that the area of the essential domestic jurisdiction of the State is not open to UN intervention under the Charter: Article 2(7). Subsequent parts of this study will show that the traditional concepts of sovereignty and independence no longer correspond to reality.

The origin and discontinuity of legal order

Sovereignty and independence are closely related and may in some contexts of international relations be seen as almost interchangeable.[12] But what is the relative independence of a State, in which the legal order has an external origin, or where there has been a discontinuity of constitutional authority—some kind of revolution or rebellion?

In some Commonwealth countries there have been doubts as to whether the transfer of power has been complete, when independence has been established by a constitutive Act of the Westminster Parliament; and there may be impatience with 'entrenched provisions' in such an Act, which circumscribe the power of the newly independent country to make constitutional changes or even adopt particular legislation.

Further, discontinuity in the legal order of a country brought about by foreign occupation, revolution or secession can raise questions of international recognition of regimes. The previously established public authorities may be wholly displaced, but a legal order may be deemed to continue, so that the State, as the personification of that order, is still regarded internationally as existing and independent. So the Foreign Office certificate, presented to the courts on the status of Germany in 1945,[13] stated that:

1. Under paragraph 5 of the preamble to the Declaration dated June 5, 1945, of the unconditional surrender of Germany, the Governments of the UK, USA, USSR and France, assumed 'supreme authority with respect to Germany, including all the powers possessed by the German Government, the High Command, and any State, municipal or local government or authority.' The assumption for the purposes stated of the said authority did not effect the annexation of Germany.
2. In consequence of this Declaration, Germany still exists as a State, and German nationality as a nationality, but the Allied Control Commission is the agency through which the government of Germany is carried on.

In short, the status of Germany as a recognized State having a legal order was not affected by the total replacement of its governmental agents by foreign occupants; and this was emphasized by the fact that the 'unconditional surrender' of Germany had to be regarded, paradoxically perhaps, as still a sovereign act of the German State. Similarly after the unilateral declaration of independence in Southern Rhodesia, the Judicial Committee in referring to it had in mind questions that might be put: is the Smith regime the effective government of Southern Rhodesia, given its full control of the territory, or can the UK claim recognition as the effective government[14] given that the Southern Rhodesia Act (1965) had reversed the constitutional position of the territory to its pre-1923 colonial status? The Judicial Committee observed that 'The British Government, acting for the lawful sovereign, is taking steps to regain control and it is impossible to predict with certainty whether or not it will succeed',[15] but that in any case the legislative authority of Parliament was overriding.

The determination of the legal validity of acts and decisions of a constitutionally illegal regime is more difficult for its courts: it may be said that they are not competent to make the determination at all, since they are part of the illegal regime; or they may regard it as their duty to uphold 'the rule of law' and to validate at least those acts of the new administration which plainly serve public order and the general interest. The first question arises where the courts have survived the change of regime without displacement or reduction of competence, which was the case in the courts of Southern Rhodesia. The second arises where the new order continues and there is no prospect of further changes. Both arose in the courts of Southern Rhodesia after 1965; and the Appellate Division finally held that there was no prospect of British rule becoming effectively established, and that the Smith regime must be regarded as the legitimate government of Southern Rhodesia.[16]

Thus confrontations between law and power bear on the effectiveness of the legal order of a country. Kelsen has said that: 'A national legal order begins to be valid as soon as it has become, on the whole, efficacious, and ceases to be valid as soon as it loses this efficacy.' The enactment of the Southern Rhodesia Act (1965), and the decision of the Judicial Committee concerning it, were attempts to carry the law beyond the limits of its effectiveness, in treating the territory of Southern Rhodesia as part of the legal order of the United Kingdom.

1 International Contexts of Law and Power

To try now to understand the contexts in which law and power operate in international relations between the recognized units, we shall describe in turn the principal units and operators; some principal objectives of policy; and the place of law in international society.

The units and operators

Most of the land-mass of the world, with marginal seas and air-space, is at present occupied by approximately 150 nation-states, each identifiable in relation to a particular territory under organized government. To the extent that none of them are wholly isolated, politically and economically, they may be said metaphorically to form the international society of individual members or units. This notion of an international society or system leads to some simplifications and economy of thought about international relations, which is convenient and in many contexts accurate. But it is a notion that must be used with care. For contemporary international relations cannot be reduced to those of an uneasy club of Machiavellian princes, whose ambitions and fears, conflicts and collaboration, come to be described in almost personal terms; further, it must be repeated that the name of a country, or the term 'the State' refers not to a particular thing or person, but to a number of related objects, varying with the context of the proposition in which the name or term occurs. So, for example, in the simple propositions: 'China has a population of over 800 million'; 'China is a Communist country'; China has always been a Permanent Member of the Security Council'; 'China will become expansionist', the term 'China' varies in meaning and complexity, and so the propositions themselves vary greatly in the degree to which they can be taken as true or adequate statements.

Again, the society of nation-states cannot yet be said to form a political community. Take first their number, which is minute compared with the population of even the smallest community forming a nation-state. The society lacks the pressures of cohesion which numbers impose on a large society; at best there are coordinations of policy in contrast to the regular and necessary subordination of individual policies to a common interest. Again the differences of size and power, by whatever criteria these are measured, are vastly greater between nation-states than between human beings. Hobbes remarked that 'Nature has made man so equal in the faculties of body and mind . . . [that] the weakest has strength enough to kill the strongest', and Hedley Bull has, by analogous reasoning, pointed out that the society of nation-states, given its extreme inequalities, has to tolerate more anarchy than a national community, for there is in that society no monopoly or centralization of cohesion or force comparable to that found in a community.

Can these inequalities be quantified, and the standing and behaviour of nation-states in their mutual relations statistically measured? The selection and 'weighting' of the component factors is obviously difficult, but an example may be considered which appears not unrealistic.[17] Here five criteria have been adopted with different weighting: GNP; GNP per capita; population; nuclear weapon capacity; prestige. GNP was measured at 1965 prices in units of 1 billion, and rated from 1 to 4. Population is rated from 0 to 5 corresponding to populations ranging from under 2 million to those over 250 million. Nuclear weapon capacity goes from 0 to 3, 2 representing the possession of nuclear weapons, and 3 a second-strike capacity. The criterion of prestige measures the degree of independence enjoyed by a country: it ranges from being non-independent (0) through being alliance-aligned (1), neutral or non-aligned (2), to being leader of an alliance, or actively independent in a hostile environment (3).

Power ranking by these criteria yielded the following order in 1967:

US and USSR, respectively 7 and 5 points ahead of China, France, Japan, UK, a group of equals;
Federal Republic of Germany, Italy, Canada, India, also a group of equals;
Sweden;

then groups of closely comparable countries in terms of measurement:

22

Australia, Austria, Brazil, Netherlands, Spain, Switzerland, Yugoslavia

followed by

Argentina, Belgium, Pakistan, Poland, South Africa, Czechoslovakia, Denmark, German Democratic Republic, Indonesia, Israel, Mexico.

In the result measurement and intuition are not far apart in identification of the top twenty-odd countries.

But other important units are those institutions that have an organized and permanent structure, generally called 'international organizations'. The more evolved type such as the specialized agencies of the UN and the European Communities, present analogies both with democratic forms of central government and with national corporations; while organizations such as OECD, NATO, the Warsaw Pact and the Arab League rather resemble clubs. So the Assembly or Conference of the member states of a UN specialized agency is similar to a Parliament or a shareholders' meeting; the Executive Board or Committee is like a Council of Ministers or Cabinet, or the board of directors of a company—the actual designation of the Executive Boards of the IMF and IBRD; and the Secretariat functions as a central civil service, or the managerial staff of a company.

A further common feature is that of legal personality. Usually an international organization, a central government so far as it is in action identifiable with the State, and a company, are corporate bodies seen as distinct from their participating members. So in English law a corporation aggregate is: 'a collection of individuals united in one body under a special denomination, having perpetual succession under an artificial form, and vested . . . with the capacity of acting in several respects as an individual . . . according to the design of its institutions or the powers conferred upon it.' Mention must then be made here of the international influence and, in some contexts, power of public and transnational private corporations, engaged in finance, trade, manufactures, and extraction of resources; and of the latter there are at least three kinds. First, there are groups of enterprises, operating on a large scale—perhaps of $100 million or more of annual sales—and coordinated virtually by one private, nationally registered company; the coordination is achieved through foreign subsidiaries or holding companies, wholly or partly owned

23

by the national company. The main purpose of coordination will be to spread financial and trade risks, to obtain tax benefits, to secure the benefits of widespread common services—in sales, exports and imports, research and development—and to secure the supply of raw materials and direct the sales of products. Such groups of enterprises are commonly known as multinational corporations.

Two or more companies may also be coordinated horizontally by mergers or joint management, or to a lesser degree for such purposes as the sharing of profits or research and development. These combinations may be called transnational enterprises, though the practical differences between them and multinational corporations are probably only those of legal structure and scale of operations.

An international company proper may be distinct again in that, though usually incorporated for convenience in one country, it is established to perform an international public service: examples are the Suez Canal Company; the Bank for International Settlements; Eurofima; Eurochemie; and the Société de Fluoration de l'Uranium, the last three being European institutions.

The role of the multinational corporations in the contemporary world resembles in some ways that of early British enterprises such as the East India Company and British South Africa Corporation in that, given the scale of their operations, they may perform quasi-state functions.

We have briefly described the units. As has been already remarked, the *operators* in international relations within the units described are in the end individual human beings, acting usually in some kind of combination. Among those to whom power or influence in the conduct of international relations may be in varying degrees attributed, whether as practitioners or observers, are heads of State; Ministers; members of Parliament; civil servants, national and international; managers of corporations; technical advisers, journalists; political scientists. Legal advisers, judges and jurists will also have roles in law-making and law-observance in international relations. Some explanations may be given here of the adoption of the term 'practitioner', and of the role of legal advisers.

The term 'practitioner' is to be preferred to 'decision-maker' for two reasons. First, to call the formation of national policy, and its execution in domestic or international contexts, a decision-making process is altogether too simplified and complacent a judgement of it; for the process is carried on under harsh domestic and external pressures and constraints, often with incomplete information and conflicting advice, and in face of the all-too-frequent emergence of the unexpected—Thucydides considered the incalculable, the unpredictable, to be the major, even decisive, factor in politics. Theodore Sorensen has emphasized[18] that: '... the essence of decision is choice; and to choose, it is first necessary to know ... But several policies, all good, may conflict. Several means, all bad, may be all that are open.' So there are 'organic limits on decision-making, of permissibility, available resources, available time, previous commitments, and available information'.

Secondly, only seldom are decisions or their makers capable of certain identification; the whole is a process involving many, not an act of one, though in every system of government there must be a point where, in the words of President Truman, 'the buck stops'.

Indeed it may be asked how often decisions are taken in the higher levels of government, which can be really called clear and free choices.

The role of legal advisers to the practitioners of government in foreign affairs has been described by high authority in the nineteenth century in terms which are still apt today. Lord Selborne said that legal advisers must confine themselves to questions of law without meddling with policy, and that: 'Our duty as Law Officers was to tell the Government as far as we could not what was expedient, nor what we might on abstract principles think a good rule, as between belligerents and neutrals, but what was actually the rule established by the conduct and usage and acceptance of civilized nations, or by any law or usage binding between ourselves and the United States, according to which the act of our Government, as neutral in this context [the American civil war], ought to be determined.' Lord Selborne, Lord Chancellor from 1872 to 1874 and 1880 to 1885, had been a law officer from 1861 to 1866. Lord Westbury was a law officer as Sir Richard Bethell from 1852 to 1858, and as Lord Chancellor advised a newly appointed Queen's Advocate in 1862 thus: 'Eschew long opinions, and much-reasoned opinions—the authorities in office desire little beyond a clear rule of action: the opinion is not to convince; it is to guide, conduct and relieve from responsibility.'[18a]

But the law to be applied to situations, domestic or international, which is of any degree of complexity in the facts or interests involved, is rarely indisputable. While domestic legal issues may be determined by judicial or other process, which is accepted as definitive even where opinion may be divided, in international law, in the words of

Richard Falk, 'the absence of generally competent adjudicating institutions makes it very difficult to move beyond the adversary level of discourse.' In international relations, then, legal issues and arguments can often have a symbolic or tactical role seldom to be found in domestic law.

Some objectives of policy

The practitioners of government, including technical advisers, work in international relations in a stream of events, some of which exhibit continuity and pattern over time, others being novel or incalculable in their consequences. To the first there may be a patterned response in that an appropriate policy or response will already have been designed, and corresponding action taken or avoided, as policy may indicate; but there is also the possibility that policy can become stereotyped and disoriented from an evolving situation. For the second, policy and action must be improvised, though some guiding principles may be available. In both circumstances the time-scale of events can determine the response and its effectiveness.

So events or situations may constitute a crisis, compelling immediate action, or calling for action or inaction over a short term, or for a planned policy to be executed over time. How long is immediate or short term varies of course: in an unexpected confrontation of nuclear weapons, immediate could be twenty minutes or less, while in the Suez crisis, the response to the Egyptian nationalization of the Suez Canal Company took over three months; many international crises, so called, are really symptoms of some organic conflicts or weaknesses, as in the present energy 'crisis'.

In the last two centuries some guiding ideas and principles have come to be recognized, applied with varying success, and sometimes discarded, in the conduct of international relations; and law has had a distinct part in both their formulation and their use. We may briefly describe them here but shall be returning to them in the succeeding chapters. As conceived, and if consistently applied, these ideas and principles would together and at the same time enable each country to pursue and secure its own national interests; make possible avoidance or resolution of the sometimes inevitable conflicts between those interests; and extend international cooperation where common, even global, interests are involved.

The notion of *vital interests* was graphically expressed in the UK reservation to the Briand-Kellogg Pact (1928),[19] stating that:

There are certain regions of the world the welfare and integrity of which constitute a special and vital interest for our peace and safety. His Majesty's Government have been at pains to make it clear in the past that interference with these regions cannot be suffered. Their protection against attack is to the British Empire a measure of self-defence. It must be clearly understood that His Majesty's Government in Great Britain[20] accept the new treaty upon the distinct understanding that it does not prejudice their freedom of action in this respect.

The United States, in a note circulated during the preparation of the Pact, declared that:

Every nation is free at all times and regardless of treaty provisions to defend its territory from attack or invasion, and it alone is competent to decide whether circumstances require recourse to war in self-defence.

Other countries made similar reservations: for example, Japan reserved 'a right of self-defence' and South Africa 'the natural right of legitimate self-defence'. The interest of the Pact lies not only in these reservations but in the distinction it suggests between legal and political obligation.

The reservations bring together a number of principles: vital interests, spheres of influence, non-intervention, and self-defence against intervention; further, the US expressly and the British reservation implicitly claim an exclusive right to determine whether, in given circumstances, action including war is necessary for self-defence. Finally, the British reservation is not confined to national territory, but claims vital interests in the condition of various regions of the world. Some critical questions are posed to which we shall return later.

As regards non-intervention, how far can the essentially domestic jurisdiction of a country reach?[21] Can self-defence anticipate intervention, or is self-defence sometimes itself an intervention or form of aggression? In any case, who is to decide whether the vital interests of a country are in issue, when it invokes them to justify recourse to use of armed force or economic coercion, and whether the measures taken are proportionate? To the last question the International Military Tribunal at Nuremberg replied:

Whether action taken under the claim of self-defence was in fact aggressive or defensive must ultimately be subject to investigation and adjudication, if international law is ever to be enforced.[22]

For the moment, we may draw one of two conclusions about the Pact. A legal conclusion might be that the reservations were incompatible with the object and purpose of the Pact, which was the renunciation of war, and that the countries making such reservations could not then be regarded as effective parties to it;[23] and further that there cannot be an agreement, binding in law, where a party is left free to disregard its terms on conditions to be later determined by that party alone.[24]

The other conclusion, to be preferred as more realistic and in the long run more constructive, is that the Pact was a statement of political, rather than legal obligations. It made no provision for its objective and independent interpretation, and it was hardly capable of enforcement in the last resort save by measures, which it itself forbade. Further, governments may understandably have recourse to the solemnity and charisma of a treaty between heads of States, as no more than a symbolical expression of common aspirations. The Helsinki Final Act was in great part similar, for particular care was taken not to regard it as a formal treaty, despite frequent references to existing rights and obligations of States; so

> The participating States note . . . that the present Declaration [on Principles guiding Relations between Participating States] does not affect their rights and obligations, nor the corresponding treaties and other agreements and arrangements;

and,

> . . . this Final Act . . . is not eligible for registration under Article 102 of the Charter of the UN.[25]

It is more constructive in the long run to deny legal status to instruments such as the Briand-Kellogg Pact or contemporary declarations of a right of self-determination of peoples, since it can reduce public misunderstanding and disillusion about international law and its effectiveness, and it can at the same time enhance the role of political obligation in international relations. The political obligations of States are parallel to the moral obligations of individuals, and may sometimes have the same content and purpose; and the forces which cause them to be performed or disregarded will be often not wholly unlike those that govern the behaviour of individuals.

Membership of the UN involves a number of political obligations, such as the peaceful settlement of international disputes: Article 2(3), and the pursuit of policies such as will raise standards of living, secure full employment, and make progress in social and economic development: Articles 55(a) and 56. These and other political obligations are not the less compelling because they cannot be characterized as legal obligations. We shall illustrate this distinction later.

The *balance of power* is a process rather than a condition of inter-State relations. It was described by von Gentz in 1806:[26] 'The balance of power perhaps would have been with more propriety called a system of counterpoise, for perhaps the highest of its results is not so much a perfect equipoise as a constant alternate vacillation in the scales of the balance, which from the application of counterweights is prevented from ever passing certain limits.' Lord Palmerston, linking the maintenance of a balance of power with self-preservation, also described it in the House of Commons in 1854 as meaning that 'a number of weaker States may unite to prevent a stronger one from acquiring a power that should be dangerous to them, and which should overthrow their independence, their liberty and their freedom of action.'

The balance of power was a prime factor in international relations in the eighteenth and nineteenth centuries; and given that many of the factors are variable—particularly the economic and geopolitical —it may be that a balance can be maintained, and therefore sought as a goal of policy, only in stable conditions over limited periods of time.[27] The recognizable balances of power are bipolar, where a great power is opposed for self-protection by an alliance of weaker countries, or two great powers are so opposed, each supported by weaker allies. Here the balance may be maintained by the principle of collective security, that an attack upon one is an attack upon all.[28] But where there is in fact multipolarity of power, the multiplication of factors may put such a balance beyond the margin of description, and even beyond practical policy choices. Here the notion of 'peaceful coexistence' may enter in,[29] though it has its ambiguities, differing much in its use on the one hand by Khrushchev from 1961, and as an expression on the other of UN Charter principles. Equivalent were the 'five principles' (*pancha sila*) adopted in the China-India Treaty (1954) as governing trade and relations between 'the Chinese region of Tibet' and India: mutual respect for sovereignty and territorial integrity; non-aggression; non-interference in internal affairs; equality; mutual interests.

29

The legal overtones of some of these principles prompt the question as to what part law has in the balance of power.

The legal fiction of the equality of States, expressed in Article 2(1) of the UN Charter, can hardly accommodate a balance of power, as the Charter itself recognized in giving to five States, visibly selected in terms of a balance of power, each a right of veto on its decisions. However, the law has provided means of structuring at least two elements in the balance of power: spheres of influence and power frontiers.

The term *sphere of influence* has, like 'suzerainty', 'protection', 'paramountcy' and 'dependence', the imprecision which is both a weakness and strength of political concepts. These terms, now almost obsolete, have been loose descriptions of special relationships between countries or between countries and regions, in which there has been a substantial power difference. The relationships range from political, economic or military influence, recognized but varying in degree, up to formal subordination, hardly distinguished in practice from annexation. A sphere of influence lies in the penumbra of power, and its character and limits have been often left indeterminate. So the Berlin Conference on Africa in 1884 recognizing the establishment of the Congo Free State, placed it and the Congo River under a treaty regime, but the control of the upper basin of the Niger River was still left to France, and of the lower basin to Britain. Further, the Berlin Act (1885), which embodied these arrangements, declared that territorial claims in the coastal regions of Africa must depend for recognition on the traditional rule of effective occupation. But the European powers were interested less in territorial annexations in central and southern Africa than the benefits of commercial penetration left in practice to the trading corporations. An illustration of a sphere of influence being gradually given a legal structure is in the South Africa Offences Act (1863), enacted by the Westminster Parliament; it provided that the criminal law of the Cape Colony be applicable to all British subjects

> within any territory in Africa being to southward of the 25th degree of south latitude, and not being within the jurisdiction of any civilized government

and the Act expressly excluded

> any claim or title whatsoever to dominion or sovereignty over any such territory as aforesaid . . . or any derogation from the rights of

30

the tribes or people, inhabiting such territory, or chiefs or rulers, to any such sovereignty or dominion.[30]

The sphere of influence principle is also expressed in the British declaration, terminating the protected status of Egypt in 1922, that:

> HM Government . . . recognise Egypt as an independent sovereign state, while preserving for future agreements between Egypt and themselves, certain matters in which the interests and obligations of the British Empire are involved . . . [and] will regard as an unfriendly act any attempt at interference in the affairs of Egypt by another power.[31]

Such large land territories or groups of islands, inhabited by loosely associated or mutually hostile, tribes or groups, each with its own forms of social rule, were said to be under the protection of one of the powers. This protection had legal structures, a common feature of which was that the protecting state was recognized as having exclusive control of the external relations, particularly in trade and defence of the territory under protection. But there was a constitutional difference between protected States and protectorates. Protected States were territories under a single often autocratic ruler, with whom a formal agreement was concluded, providing essentially for the transfer to the protecting State of all external relations and responsibility. Such 'treaties of protection' would often also provide for special status and privileges, and separate courts for traders, and even for a right of intervention by the protecting State to maintain internal order. The Permanent Court of International Justice said of such arrangements:[32]

> The extent of the powers of a protecting State in the territory of a protected State depends, first, upon the treaties between [them] and secondly, upon the conditions under which the protectorate has been recognised by third Powers as against whom there is an intention to rely on the provisions of the treaties.

The status and domestic jurisdiction of the ruler are then legally preserved, and the International Court of Justice observed of the Treaty of Fez (1912), under which Morocco became a protected State of France, that Morocco, even under protection, retained its personality as a State in international law.[33]

In the British system protected States were established largely in the Malayan peninsula, the Indian sub-continent—nearly seven hundred native States—and the Persian Gulf. Protectorates were established in areas, mainly in Africa and the Pacific, where there might be several communities each having its own chiefs or forms of social rule, but no single ruler.[34] In protectorates, then, not only was there external responsibility of the protecting State but it would also exercise in practice exclusive administrative authority over the territory, in which the various communities acquiesced: called colonial protectorates in British practice, they differed from colonies only in not forming part of 'HM dominions', so that their inhabitants were not British subjects; but like those of protected States they were internationally recognized as 'British protected persons'.

While protected States and protectorates have been, at least in their origins, ways of establishing or securing spheres of influence, they were of course relatively limited in size territorially, and became over time hardly distinguishable from colonies.

But spheres of influence are generally both politically and territorially larger, and between them or between regions involved in a balance of power there can be seen to be *power frontiers*.[35] These seldom coincide with territorial boundary lines, and differ also from them in that, while boundary lines are generally permanent, power frontiers appear, shift and dissolve over time. They are perhaps best described as areas of inward or outward pressure between two spheres of influence, large or small. A power frontier may be political or strategic or both, and it will be also geophysically determined. So on land it may be a single city like Berlin or Trieste, or a group of adjacent countries as in Central Europe or South East Asia, or a chain of countries with or without common frontiers such as Turkey, Iran, Pakistan, Afghanistan. On the seas it will be found at critical points or areas of communication such as the North West approaches, the Straits of Gibraltar, the Dardanelles, the Suez Canal and the Malay Straits. The strategic uses of air and outer space have greatly altered some power frontiers, and have perhaps, at some levels of power exercise, removed them.

Where a power frontier is in close geographical proximity to both centres of power, strategic forces will predominate so that intervention in or over the 'frontier' will be likely to precipitate some degree of armed conflict. Such intervention may be seen as inward towards a power centre and denounced as aggressive, or as outward from a power centre and claimed as defensive. Where the frontier is geographically remote from at least one of the power centres, the forces at work will be primarily political rather than strategic; but the ambiguities are illustrated by the boundary incident in July 1979 between the USSR and China, in which two soldiers were killed and which occurred soon after the proposal by China for talks with the USSR to establish normal relations. Was the seemingly exaggerated reaction, both angry and public, to the incident by the USSR political or strategic: to compromise or influence the talks, or to reflect Soviet concern with boundary security?

In a secular view a power frontier may be at one time intensely active while at other times it may be stable and quiescent, or it may disappear. Further, countries situated on a power frontier can themselves affect the movements of power by alignment with one power centre or another, or may by a policy of negotiation seek to avoid becoming part of a power frontier at all.

The enunciation and application of the Monroe doctrine make it a classic model of power frontiers. Largely drafted by John Quincy Adams, the annual message of President Monroe to Congress in December 1823 stated that: '... The American continents, by the free and independent condition which they have assumed and maintained, are henceforth not to be considered as subjects for future colonisation by any European power ...' but that '... with the existing colonies or dependencies of any European power we have not interfered and shall not interfere ...' However, 'We could not view any interposition for the purpose of suppressing them or controlling in any other manner their destiny, by any other European power, in any other light than as a manifestation of an unfriendly disposition towards the United States.'

In 1904 President Roosevelt said that: 'Chronic wrongdoing, or an impotence which results in a general loosening of the ties of civilised society, may in America as elsewhere ultimately require the intervention by some civilised nation and in the western hemisphere the adherence of the United States to the Monroe doctrine may force the United States, however reluctantly, in flagrant cases of such wrongdoing or impotence, to the exercise of an international police power'; and in 1915 President Wilson applied this principle to the control or suppression of manipulation of economic interests when, in defending United States intervention in Haiti, he declared that: 'The Government of the United States regards it as one of the grave possibilities of certain sorts of concessions granted by governments in America to European financiers and contractors, and of certain sorts of contracts entered into by those governments with European banking houses and financiers that the legitimate and natural course of enforcing

B   33

claims might lead to measures, which would imperil the political independence or, at least, the complete political autonomy of the American states involved.' What has been called the Carter doctrine is similar, expressed by the President after the Russian intervention in Afghanistan: 'An attempt by any outside force to gain control of the Persian Gulf region will be regarded as an assault on the vital interests of the United States. It will be repelled by use of any means necessary, including military force.' How far the United States had been actively protecting these vital interests is questionable.

But these statements together lay down two principles for maintaining the stability of a power frontier: first, intervention from the opposing power centre in the frontier area, by exploitation of political weakness, territorial bases or economic interests, must be prevented; and secondly, intervention in a frontier country from the neighbouring power centre is permissible, if its political independence is threatened by weakness of government or subversion of order.

The law has again provided, in addition to systems of protection, means of stabilizing power frontiers by forms of international regime, and certain general rules. The international regimes are based on formal agreements, providing any necessary administrative structures for the area concerned, and secured by sanctions of varying character and efficacy. So after the First World War a power frontier, to be put to severe test in the Second World War, came to be established with a legal structure in the Near and Middle East by a linkage of international regimes, including mandates and protectorates. It can be seen as running from the Dardanelles, placed under an international regime, comprising demilitarization and rights of passage by the Treaty of Lausanne (1923), through the mandates over Syria, Lebanon, Iraq, Palestine and Transjordan, the protectorate over Egypt, and the Anglo-Egyptian condominium over the Sudan. Characteristically the 'frontier' underwent changes between the two world wars, but the essential structure was preserved. Britain retained by treaty with Egypt, after its independence in 1922, and with Iraq after termination of the mandate in 1932, bases and a military presence in both countries; and the Montreux Convention (1936), though favouring Turkey, did not take away the international status of the Dardanelles. The principle of non-aggression, which has come to be recognized as a rule of international law, is also applied to the protection of spheres of influence. The UN Charter, Article 2(4) imposes an obligation on member States to refrain, in their international relations, from the threat or use of force against the territorial integrity or political independence of any State. The distinction between the threat or use of force across national boundaries and, less directly, against political independence is important; for what is prohibited includes the threat or use of force aimed at breaking the political alignment or non-alignment of a country, in order to destabilize a sphere of influence.

Collective security has been developed since the end of the First World War as a means of protecting vital interests, maintaining a balance of power, and securing power frontiers, and its roots are old. For it is based upon a group of countries having a common interest in achieving such purposes and a will to associate in order to do so. The preservation of such groups both from internal subversion and external attack has been the concern of the Holy Alliance and Concert of Powers in the nineteenth century, and of NATO and the Warsaw Pact in our own times; and the League Covenant and the UN Charter have attempted to generalize the idea; while the latter in Article 51 expressly recognizes a right of 'collective self-defence'.

The objectives of *common interest* may influence and determine policy such as the freedom of trade and payments and the protection of the environment; and these come together in the management of the access to and use of natural resources.

Finally, the protection of human rights and freedoms has become both an instrument of foreign policy, and a goal of collective action.

The place of law in international society

Let us start with the polarization of law and power. Here political forces are seen as determinative and the view of what is or what should be the law is wholly subjective; and consequently law is at best a servant of power and at worst a mere whitewashing of policy. So according to H. J. Morgenthau: 'Foreign policy like all politics is in its essence a struggle for power, waged by sovereign nations for material advantage.'[36] Conflict must then be seen in terms of relative power, and not 'conceived in absolute terms of peace, law and order vs. aggression, crime and anarchy'. Moral judgements are therefore irrelevant, diplomatic negotiation being the only instrument to reduce conflict. Coral Bell has remarked that 'many of the more successful modes of [crisis] management have been strikingly non-legal, even anti-legal, in quality.'[36a]

Schwarzenberger expresses a not dissimilar view: 'The primary function of law is to assist in maintaining the supremacy of force and the hierarchies established on the basis of power, and to give to this overriding system the respectability and sanctity law confers.'[37] But the upholding of peace, law and order against subversion and aggression, regarded by Morgenthau as unrealistic, may also be seen as simply a means of avoiding change, since the maintenance of the existing order, including any legal structure it may have, is in the interest of the holders of power. So Marxism in its pure form would say that the rules and standards of international law, as they have evolved since the mid-nineteenth century, have simply served capitalist expansion and the maintenance of the capitalist system as a centre of power. For Rosa Luxemburg imperialism was the political form of a competitive struggle to keep hold of precapitalist countries as the last remaining sources of capital; and Bukharin predicted conflict between these precapitalist countries, when they attained independence, and the old capitalist societies, with which they would want to compete.[38]

But no State is an island. There have always been and had to be transnational contacts between them, and the formation and function of law in international relations are subtler and more complicated than these polarizations of law and power suggest. Grotius held that: '. . . law is not founded on expediency alone. There is no State so powerful that it may not some time need the help of others outside itself, either for purposes of trade or even to ward off the forces of many foreign nations united against it. . . . All things are uncertain the moment men depart from law.'[39] So latterday Marxists have conceded that general international law is 'the international code of peaceful coexistence', though ideally it is still to be ultimately transformed into socialist international law for a community of classless societies.[40]

There is in fact an organic interdependence of States, which traditional international law has itself had difficulty in recognizing. For there is an obvious contradiction between the proposition that law entails the subordination of those subject to it, and the proposition that States are subjects of international law, but still sovereign and independent. Hegel considered that: 'The relation between States is a relation between autonomous entities, which make natural stipulations, but which are at the same time superior to these stipulations.' Anzilotti, writing in 1913, made a similar approach when he said that the principle *pacta sunt servanda*—treaties must be observed—is derived from nothing else than the collective will of States.

If, then, being superior to the stipulations it makes means that a

State is free to disregard them—compare the Briand-Kellogg Pact—
or if agreements between States are to be kept only because there is
an agreement between States to keep them, we have only either
contradiction or tautology. It was perhaps some such consideration
that led Anzilotti later to describe the principle *pacta sunt servanda*
as 'a primary norm, over and above which there is no other norm,
that could explain it juridically, and which the science of law nevertheless accepts as a hypothesis or an undemonstrable postulate'.[41]

But apart from the fact that what cannot be demonstrated is not a
matter of science, these and like attempts to find some primary
norms, some higher rules, to explain the observance of international
law, are searching for what is not needed or is not there. There can be
said to be international legal order, because the formation and observance of certain rules and standards, both nationally and in international relations, meet in fact certain political, social, or economic
needs of nation-states. The legal order, composed of these rules and
standards, is neither higher in some moral sense than the political
order, nor is it separate from it; it is an organic part of international
society. In short, the international legal order is a matter of fact, not
of theory or principle.

Games illustrate this kind of legal order, not because international
relations can be seen as forms of game, as some theorists appear to
suggest, but because games express certain human characteristics
and habits, which are also operative in international relations. So
the 'rules of the game', whether at cards or on the football field or in
international trade, can secure stability and order by limiting behaviour and making it reasonably predictable. Further, the 'rules'
may recognize both the elements of chance—the 'deal', the 'joker',
the throw of the dice, the emergency exceptions—and also the factors
of cooperation—the 'partners', the 'team', the cartel, and the allies.
Finally, non-observance of the rules may bring penalties or at least
injure the image of the player or operator among his fellows.

Some of what has been suggested about political community is
applicable to the society of nation-states (*Staatengesellschaft*), though
it does not yet constitute an international community (*Weltgemein-
schaft*). There is a will to associate, expressed, however, not in
subordination to one authority with a systematized distribution of
law-making power, but in coordinate and politically still inchoate
forms: defence alliances, economic unions, and other forms of international organization. There is also a visible will to dissociate both
within and between nation-states, expressed in claims of self-

determination and policies of neutralism, non-alignment or conflict. There is also no common territorial base, though Antarctica, the deep sea-bed and Earth satellite orbits may be the beginning. But law in international society has some characteristics in common with law in a political community. In both it is expressed in sets of propositions varying in precision, direction and authority, so that the law applicable to given situations, will vary in form and effectiveness and be often a matter of dispute. But law is always institutional, and if we set out a rough pattern of the institutionalized forms of international relations the role of law will begin to be seen:

Purposes	Structures	Methods	Instruments
Consultation	'Ad hoc' conference	Diplomatic exchanges	Recommendations
	Regular conferences		Adoption of standards
Resolution of particular conflicts		Organized persuasion	
	Administrative bodies		Directives
Systematic collaboration		Supervision	Decisions
Regulation and management	Permanent intergovernmental organization	Authorization	
		Mandatory decision	Regimes

To elucidate the pattern, it may be said first that the degree of involvement, commitment or obligation for governments increases generally towards the lower end of each column, though there is of course no systematic evolution in any of these directions; further the various components are not to be seen as directly related horizontally. So an *ad hoc* conference might establish an international regime, and continuing consultation and recommendations will be a purpose and instrument of any permanent organization; or again a particular conflict might be resolved by the establishment of a regime under international supervision.

It is useful to distinguish in the pattern the roles of law as rules and law as process. Here process is wider than procedure, which may be governed by rules. Law as rules is needed in some part at least, for example, in international regimes, for the regulation or management of trade, payments and resources, for the constitution and functioning of international organizations, and for the conduct of diplomacy. These rules are usually to be found in international agreements—the term has come to include multilateral conventions, pacts or charters, and also bilateral agreements and exchanges of notes. These instruments may, like statutes, contain regulations, commands and prohibitions, which the participating countries accept as obligatory. Bilateral agreements, concluded between pairs of such countries, on such matters as mutual trade and payments, boundary settlements, cultural exchanges, extradition, are essentially contracts, while multilateral agreements, such as conventions on the law of the sea, or diplomatic immunities, or the treatment of prisoners of war, though still contractual in form, may be the beginning of international legislation, hence the distinction that has been made between *traité-contrat* and *traité-loi*.

Regularities of behaviour also come to be established in many areas, governed by 'rules of the game' or 'gentlemen's agreements'; and conformity with them is expected and relied upon by all participants. Systematic collaboration may lead them to making arrangements, adoption of standards, or operating methods, the last being sometimes incorporated into domestic law, as for example diplomatic immunities developed in customary international law. Trade usages, involving the observance of common standards, without the compulsion of legal rules, may still function in effect as law, because of their regularity and predictability. So in the United States Uniform Commercial Code, adopted in a large number of States of the Union, a trade usage is aptly defined as:

> any practice or method of dealing having such regularity of observance as to justify an expectation that it will be observed with respect to the transaction in question.

Law as process is then a way of describing regularities of transnational behaviour between various units, public and private.

The probability of law observance, and the relation of law and power, in international relations depend then on a number of factors; and while the disregard of particular rules or standards or regularities of behaviour may not be frequent, it can be dangerous when it does happen or is threatened. So Elihu Root observed that: 'It is only for the occasional non-conformist that the sheriff and the policeman are kept in reserve; and it is only because the non-conformists are occasional and comparatively few in number that the sheriff and the policeman have any effect at all.'[42] But where are the international sheriff and policeman, and what are the sanctions of law in international relations?

To determine the incidence and effectiveness of law in the conduct of international relations and the exercise of power, we again construct a kind of matrix:

Authority	Influence and coercion
National interests	Common objectives

Before describing these components in more detail, we may explain the matrix analogy in a few brief propositions:

Power is the capacity to exercise influence or use coercion in a national interest or to secure common objectives of nation-states;

Law, as rules or standards or regularity of behaviour, has authority to the extent that the rights and obligations based on it are recognized as such because it has an institutionalized source, or its observance secures common objectives, or both;

The components will vary in magnitude, and their respective magnitudes must be at least approximately known for an assessment to be made of the impact of law on the exercise of power in a given international context;

Typical patterns of conduct of international relations that may emerge are:

national interests are served by influence or coercion, law being disputed or disregarded;

national interests are served by influence, supported or justified by conventional or customary international law;

common objectives are achieved by influence or coercion;

common objectives are achieved through some institutionalized authority;

authority is maintained by coercion.

Authority in international relations takes forms similar to those of domestic authority, namely rules or standards or regularity of behaviour, which are in some way institutionalized. Indeed a striking feature of international relations since 1920 has been the progressive institutionalization of working arrangements and other means of collaboration and policy coordination between governments: examples are the UN and its specialized agencies;[43] OAS, OAU and the Council of Europe, ASEAN; NATO and the Warsaw Pact; GATT, OECD and COMECON; and the European Communities.

The UN has come to be recognized as a corporation, distinct from its members, and as a legal person on the international plane. The EEC has similarly become a participant in the GATT and may even, if some current proposals are adopted, become a party to the European Convention on Human Rights.

The UN not only has authority over and responsibility for its servants and agents,[44] but its General Assembly has some of the characteristics of a parliament in its composition, its procedures, its shifting blocs and caucuses, comparable in some ways to political parties, and in its resolutions. It is also a convenient centre for diplomatic exchanges, conducted by permanent representatives of member States, this being of particular value to small countries, unable to maintain extended diplomatic representation abroad. The General Assembly processes have been aptly described as a kind of 'parliamentary diplomacy'. What then is the authority of its recommendations or declarations?[45]

UN Charter Article 10 authorizes it to 'discuss', and to 'make recommendations to Members' on 'any questions or any matters within the scope of the present Charter'. Articles 11 and 12 elaborate this function in the maintenance of international peace and security. Article 13(1) requires the General Assembly to:

initiate studies and make recommendations for the purpose of: (a) promoting international cooperation in the political field and encouraging the progressive development of international law and its codification; (b) promoting international cooperation in the economic, social, cultural, educational, and health fields, and assisting in the realization of human rights and fundamental freedoms for all without distinction as to race, sex, language or religion.

It is plain that the General Assembly in carrying out these tasks may not go formally beyond recommendations; and such resolutions cannot therefore, by the bare act of adoption and promulgation, have the binding effect of a legislative enactment. Nevertheless there are resolutions, which may formulate standards of international conduct or policy, or may be at least declaratory of the law.[46] Examples of the first are declarations of principles on which human societies should be based: the Universal Declaration of Human Rights (Resolution 217–III: 10.12.1948); Granting of Independence to Colonial Countries and Peoples (Resolution 1514–XI: 14.12.1960);[47] Permanent Sovereignty over Natural Resources (Resolution 1803–XVII: 14.12.1962); Principles of Friendly Relations and Cooperation among States (Resolution 2625–XXV: 24.10.1970); Inadmissibility of Intervention in the Domestic Affairs of States and the Protection

41

of their Independence and Sovereignty (Resolution 2750–XXV: 17.12.1970); Charter of the Economic Rights and Duties of States (Resolution 3281–XXIX: 12.12.1974). Examples of the second are Declaration of Legal Principles governing the activities of States in the Exploration and Use of Outer Space (Resolution 1962–XVIII: 13.12.1963); Declaration of Principles governing the Seabed and Ocean Floor, and the Subsoil thereof, beyond the Limits of National Jurisdiction (Resolution 2749–XXV: 17.12.1970); and, in the field of armaments, the declaration that the use in international armed conflicts of any chemical agents is contrary to international law (Resolution 2603A–XXIV: 16.12.1969) and the condemnation of all nuclear weapon tests (Resolution 2828A–XXVI: 16.12.1971). The General Assembly has also had recourse in this field to the drafting of international conventions for adoption by States: for example, Treaty on the Prohibition of the Emplacement of Nuclear Weapons and other Weapons of Mass Destruction on the Seabed (Resolution 2660–XXV: 7.12.1970), while Resolution 3264–XXIX: 9.12.1974 expressed the intent to draft a convention prohibiting action to influence the environment and climate for military and other hostile purposes.

The authority of these resolutions can be measured in part by the size and distribution of votes. A resolution adopted unanimously must obviously carry more weight than one where there is a number of negative votes or abstentions. But numbers cannot alone be decisive; so a resolution adopted after the UN had come to include the great majority of countries of the world must be more representative of opinion and authoritative than earlier resolutions; further, a small minority of powerful countries may put the authority of a resolution in question.

With these qualifications let us look at the voting on the resolutions. Taking first the resolutions concerned with common human interests, we see that there were no negative votes and relatively few abstentions. So on Resolution 217 (the Universal Declaration), carried 48–0–8, the whole General Assembly voted and only eight countries abstained, the USSR and its associates on the plea that the Resolution did not go far enough, and Egypt and Saudi Arabia over difficulties about rights for women. But the political impact of the Universal Declaration, embodied as its provisions were in many constitutions of newly independent countries, was far greater than its drafters could have expected, and so reflects in some degree the authority of the UN; and this is perhaps confirmed by the fact, that not only did all the abstainers vote for the resolutions in 1966,[48]

42

adopting the much more elaborate Civil and Political Rights Covenant and Economic Social and Cultural Rights Covenant, but that the USSR, and its two Republics which are UN members, and other East European countries have ratified the Covenants. While ratification does not necessarily imply observance, it is a recognition at least of the authority of the Covenants; both in fact incorporate the central provision of Resolution 1514 on self-determination, which has had its own influence, and was adopted without vote.

Resolution 1962–XVIII, on outer space, was adopted unanimously and laid down broad but novel principles to govern an area of human activity, which could not be safely left to the evolution of customary rules. The Outer Space Treaty (1967), to which the US and USSR were principal parties, repeats much of the Resolution verbatim.

The authority of Resolution 3281 (Charter of Economic Rights and Duties of States) is more controversial, and will be considered below.[49]

The development and use of weapons raise, as might be expected, still greater controversy in the General Assembly. Resolutions 2603A–XXIV (16.12.1969) and 2828A–XXVI (16.12.1971) were adopted by 80–3–36 and 74–2–37 respectively. In the former the use in international armed conflicts of chemical or biological agents of warfare was condemned as contrary to international law, embodied in the Geneva Protocol (1925). Negative votes were cast by Australia, Portugal and the US, and among the large number of countries abstaining were Belgium, Canada, China, France, Israel, Japan and UK. The later Resolution sought to condemn and bring to an end *all* nuclear weapon tests, and was opposed by Albania and China, the abstainers including those countries just mentioned except Israel, as well as the US and USSR. But it is interesting to see that Resolution 32/78 (12.12.1977) expressed grave concern that, despite repeated resolutions, nuclear weapon testing had continued unabated, and was adopted by 126–2 (Albania, China)–1 (France), all other countries with nuclear capacity being in the majority.

It may be concluded from this brief survey of certain prominent resolutions that the authority of the General Assembly, in declaring rules or standards which can serve a clear and accepted common interest of nation-states, is reasonably high, but is low where there are conflicts of interest between them.

There is of course internationally no central executive authority. The Security Council has power delegated to it to take action under Articles 41 and 42 of the Charter to maintain or restore international peace and security. The action, whether measures of economic coercion or the use of armed force, must be taken by and through members of the UN, since no UN Standing Force has yet been established under Article 43. However, members have agreed under Article 25 to accept and carry out such decisions on action by the Security Council. Further, in some international organizations, and particularly specialized agencies of the UN, the executive councils or boards, composed of representatives of a limited number of member States, may be authorized to impose sanctions on members; for example, the executive board of the IMF may, on certain conditions, declare a member ineligible to use the resources of the Fund, by way of drawings, and this can have severe economic effects.[50] Within the European Communities there are also bodies established with similar legislative or administrative authority.

In no area of international relations is the gap between recognized principles, declared intentions and actual practice so great as in the judicial or arbitral settlement of disputes. Taking the Council of Europe alone, we find that over twenty bilateral agreements, for judicial or arbitral settlement of disputes or both, have been concluded bilaterally between member States, and they have adopted the multilateral Convention on Peaceful Settlement of Disputes; yet there has been virtually no use made of this machinery.

The International Court of Justice is still far from attaining a centralized judicial authority. Its compulsory jurisdiction has been recognized by barely a third of the countries of the world, and even then with reservations in many cases, which can weaken or defeat the effective exercise of its jurisdiction. Further, like all international tribunals save those established to serve 'common markets' or by special agreement, the Court must depend for the enforcement of its judgements, not upon their having automatic legal effect in the countries concerned, but upon their good faith,[51] with the possibility of ultimate recourse to the Security Council under Article 94 of the Charter. But this recourse is limited to parties in the case and is not open to the Court itself.

The forms of international authority so far described have been institutionalized by treaty, or what is sometimes described as conventional, as distinct from customary, international law. Here the terms 'treaty', 'international agreement' bilateral or multilateral, and 'international convention' are virtually synonymous. Both treaties and customary international law may in many situations themselves serve as forms of international authority; and a central purpose of

44

the following chapters will be to assess this authority by seeing how far in practice governments adjust policies to identifiable rules of customary international law, and to rules and standards set out in treaties.

National interests are for any nation-state multiple, their number and range increasing with power; and some may be seen as vital interests, already described. Prominent among them are political stability, the control of the territorial base, the use and management of natural resources, economic growth, international 'image' and prestige, and their protection by what is generally called defence. There can be conflicts between them within the nation-state so that priorities may have to be established. So, in the terminology of war-games, there may be a 'dominating strategy', the outcome of which is, by a balancing of interests, at worst equal to or possibly better than, that of any other strategy pursuing a particular interest.

Common objectives—to secure the common interests of countries, regional or global—emerge from their growing interdependence; from the wider interventions of government in most countries in economic and social fields, which lead to internationalization of policies; and from the seen needs of security from attack or subversion or loss of essential resources. Interdependence manifests itself in many forms, such as the common management of communications, commodity trade or international liquidity, the reduction of tariff and non-tariff barriers to trade, the protection of the environment and natural resources, and defence alliances. Common objectives, which interdependence generates, are sought by means of international agreements, codes of behaviour and usages, and where practicable institutional mechanisms; and in all of these law has a function.

There may also be international identification of common principles and objectives, both social and political. F. H. Hinsley[52] describes St. Pierre's project for 'a league of peace' in 1713, of which Article II declares that 'the European society' shall not concern itself about the government of any member State 'unless it be to preserve the fundamental form of it, and give speedy and sufficient assistance to the Princes in Monarchies, and to the Magistrates in Republics, against any that are seditious or rebellious'; and cites Vattel as seeing Europe as 'une espèce de République, dont les membres, indépendants mais liés par l'intérêt commun, se réunissent pour y maintenir l'Ordre et la Liberté'.[53]

Pre-eminent in recent times have been widely accepted declara-

45

tions on the prevention and control of the use of force; the principles of self-determination of peoples; human rights and freedoms; and the protection of the environment.[54] The first three are proclaimed in the UN Declaration on the Principles of International Law concerning Friendly Relations and Cooperation among States (1970).[55] Essentially an elaboration of UN Charter provisions, the Declaration is often repetitive and sometimes obscure in its qualifications, but it serves to concentrate and unify a number of political and social principles. Two of the principles are related to the use of power and influence: restraints on the use of force, and the rule against foreign intervention in internal affairs. Under the first principle following Article 2(4) of the Charter it is stated that:

> a war of aggression constitutes a crime against the peace, for which there is responsibility under international law

and 'acts of reprisal involving the use of force' are forbidden. It is further stated that:

> no territorial acquisition resulting from the threat or use of force shall be recognized as legal.

Under the second principle it is said that:

> No State or group of States has the right to intervene, directly or indirectly, for any reason whatever in the internal or external affairs of any other State,

and

> No State may use or encourage the use of economic, political or any other type of measures to coerce another State in order to obtain from it the subordination of the exercise of its sovereign rights and to secure from it advantages of any kind. . . .

The Declaration recognizes in several contexts the shift of armed conflict generally from wars between States to irregular fighting against particular regimes, which has marked the last two decades.[56]

The Helsinki Final Act (1974) restates many of the principles of the Declaration, and particularly that on non-intervention in internal affairs.

Influence and coercion, the fourth component in our matrix, can range from cultural influences, through economic pressure, to the threat of use of overt force; and tend inevitably to infringe the principle of non-intervention. Indeed domestic pressures can constrain or direct the external policies of governments, and may themselves be caused or stimulated by more or less concealed intervention from abroad in domestic affairs. Economic coercion—in the use of denial of technical, military or financial aid, the manipulation of investments, trade embargoes—has been extensively practised with varying efficiency; and it became, both in the League Covenant and the UN Charter, the initial substitute for recourse to armed force in maintenance of international order.

Law is not only a product of these four components, but its incidence and effectiveness in the conduct of international relations and in the exercise of power, are determined by them together. What is proposed, then, is to take some recent or current international exercises of power, to examine them in terms of the suggested matrix, and to try to determine the authority of the law and its effects upon them. The examples chosen will cover two broad areas: power frontiers and the uses of intervention; and the service and protection of common interests.

2 Power Frontiers

It will be helpful to consider first how adjacent States on power frontiers, already described, may be separated territorially from each other. There may be a demarcated boundary line on the ground, passing from post to post or specified physical points or defined by longitude and latitude references, the whole being based on agreement between the adjacent States. Boundaries are more often determined with less precision by reference to physical features, indicated in an agreement or by customary rules of international law. So where a river forms a natural territorial limit, the boundary may be the mid-points of the main navigable channel (Thalweg); this may not always be beyond dispute in a wide river, particularly if it is subject to change through floods and soil movements. Again, the summits or ridges of a range of mountains may be chosen as a means of delimitation, the practical limits being in the foothills or plains below.

A frontier is a broader concept, being essentially the limits which a nation-state cannot or may not effectively move. It may be a boundary line, as described above, but it can also be an area, in which there is no determined boundary line or only lines which are in dispute. In either case we may find a power frontier.

Broadly then, boundary is a physical, and frontier a political, concept; so a boundary lies between two States, while a frontier may exist between several States.

Frontiers of China

Lord Curzon, speaking of frontiers, observed that demarcation of boundary was 'an essentially modern conception . . . It would be true to say that demarcation has never taken place except under European pressure and by the intervention of European agents.'[57]

This was particularly true of China, in which Mongolia, Chinese

Turkestan (Sinkiang), Tsinghai and Tibet were ethnically distinct frontier peoples, administered as dependencies by a special department,[58] but having no internationally recognized boundaries before the middle of the nineteenth century. What indeed is striking in the evolution of the frontiers of China since the Peace of Nanking (1842), ending the Opium War, is that to support positions, and action taken in response to increasing or lessening pressures across them, there was a continuing reliance placed by Western countries on the conclusion of treaties with China, often determining boundaries, and later legal challenges by China to the validity of some of these treaties. In other words, law has been used not only to create a framework of rights and obligations for the exercise of power, strategic and political, but also to serve as a basis of challenge to that exercise. We see in fact an evolution of law itself in the process.

China has come to have a number of adjacent foreign territories: Afghanistan, Pakistan, India, Nepal, Bhutan, Burma (an old tributary), Laos, Vietnam; Macao and Hong Kong; Korea, USSR, Mongolia. The boundary with Afghanistan is only 60 miles in length; that with Pakistan extends along the part of Kashmir claimed by Pakistan in dispute with India; and that with India includes the boundary of the former Kingdom of Sikkim. The status of Taiwan, historically part of China, is at present ambiguous; and the Ryukyu Islands, formerly a tributary of China, have been retained by Japan.

A number of power frontiers of China may be discerned here: with the USSR; with the South East Asian mainland and in particular Vietnam; and with India, though it may be for the time being quiescent. Important maritime frontiers are also emerging in the East and South China Seas, involving Taiwan and adjacent islands. We shall consider the first and last of these as particularly illustrative of the role of law.

The *Sino-Soviet frontier*, much of its boundary lines determined by treaty, is in two parts. The western runs from the Afghan to the Mongolian border, with a length of about 1,400 miles. On the Russian side are the Tadzhik, Kirghiz and Kazakh SS Republics, and on the Chinese side is the Xinjiang (Sinkiang)-Uigur Autonomsou Region. The southern border of Mongolia, formerly called Outer Mongolia, runs for about 1,800 miles, and the eastern Sino-Soviet frontier then continues, in great part along the Amur and Ussuri Rivers to the Korean border, about 70 miles west of Vladivostok.

The first recorded treaty was concluded at Nerchinsk in 1689. Two rivers, Argun and Kerbetchi,[59] were used as boundaries as well as the 'summit of the mountains' (Stanovoi Range) extending from the source of the Kerbetchi to the eastern sea; the land between this range and the Uda River was to be demarcated later. China has invoked this treaty as showing, even though the eastern sector was not in fact demarcated, that

> the vast areas north of the Heilung River (Amur) south of the Outer Kingdom mountains (?Stanovoi Range) and east of the Wusuli (Ussuri) River are all Chinese territory.[60]

This statement is made to support the claim that the Treaty of Aigun (1858) was an 'unequal' treaty.

Russian expansion to the east from the seventeenth century on had brought the Kazakh steppes into the empire, and established outposts in the Amur basin by the middle of the nineteenth century; and China was then experiencing the pressure of French and British intrusion.[61] After the Opium War, the Russians sent a military force to the Amur region and founded the port of Nikolayevsk in 1859. In the following years China was disturbed by internal rebellions and entered into negotiations with Russia, which led to the Treaty of Aigun (1858).[62] It involved large territorial concessions by China, providing that:

> The left bank of the River Amur from the River Argun (Aigun) as far as the mouth of the River Amur will belong to the Russian Empire, and its right bank down as far as the River Ussuri will belong to China; the land and places situated between the River Ussuri and the sea, as they are at present will be owned in common by Russia and China until such time as the frontier between the two States may be regulated.

Navigation on the Rivers Amur, Sungari and Ussuri was to be confined to Russian and Chinese vessels; further the 'Manchu inhabitants' of 64 villages on the left bank of the Amur were to remain under Manchu administration.[63] Although the treaty did not formally call for ratification, the Manchu government refused to accept it, not least perhaps because of the ambiguity of the term 'left bank'. Was this a cession of territory adjacent to the river, or, as the use of the term 'right bank' for China could suggest, the whole region north and east of the Amur up to the Stanovoi Range, declared to belong to China, with one small area left for demarcation, in the Treaty of Nerchinsk? However, China gave way in the Treaty of Peking (1860). This Treaty, accepted by China, not only reaffirmed the provisions of the Treaty of Aigun, but removed the ambiguity by substituting for 'left bank' the words 'land situated on the left bank (to the north) of the River Amur' (Article I). Further, the region east of the Ussuri was ceded to Russia, a Commission being appointed to demarcate the boundary from Lake Hsingkai to the River Thon-men-Kiang (Article III).[64] The Treaty of Peking has been denounced as 'unequal' by China, and a number of islands in the Ussuri have been in dispute, particularly Chenpao (Damanski) where there was fighting in 1969 between Russian and Chinese troops, with heavy casualties.

The Russian right of navigation of the Amur, Sungari and Ussuri rivers had been reaffirmed by the Treaty of St. Petersburg (1881). The position appears to have remained stable for in 1951, following the Treaty of Friendship (1950), both countries concluded an agreement on navigation and construction on the main rivers and Lake Hsingkai (Khanka). It provided that navigation would follow the main channels regardless of their relation to the boundary lines fixed in the 1861 Protocol and set a commission to supervise it. But the rivers have many islands, and in particular the Ussuri, and annual flooding causes changes of course, sometimes attaching what were islands to one bank or the other. Both main channels and boundary lines can then be indeterminate. Despite a further navigation agreement in 1957 disputes continued, and in 1966 China issued regulations on navigation by foreign vessels, which in effect imposed restrictions on Russian vessels. These led later to the clashes of 1969.

Mongolia has been in itself a power frontier between Russia and China. In the eighteenth century the whole region, including what is now the Tuva Autonomous SSR, was under Manchu suzerainty, but was for long divided in practice between what came to be called Inner Mongolia, with China settlers and essentially a part of China, and Outer Mongolia, regarded as a Chinese dependency. In 1727 a treaty was concluded, under which the Sino-Russian boundary was set and partly demarcated with frontier posts from Kyakhta to the Argun River, and westwards to a pass in the Sayan Mountains.[66] No demarcation took place along the frontier of what is now the Tuva ASSR.

In the nineteenth century Outer Mongolia was a route of passage for Russia to the east and a consulate was opened at Ulan Bator in 1861, authorized by the Treaty of Peking (1860), and more consulates were established under the Treaty of St. Petersburg (1881). In 1895 China granted Russia a concession to construct a railway across Manchuria, and in 1898 the lease of Port Arthur (Lu-Ta). But after the naval defeat of Russia by Japan in 1905 and the growth of the nationalist movement in China, the latter was able to assert more influence in Outer Mongolia, and in the negotiations for the renewal of the Treaty of St. Petersburg in 1910, refused the establishment of a Russian consulate at Khobdo (Hovdo).

An anti-Chinese movement developed and in November 1911 Mongolian leaders declared the independence of Outer Mongolia. However subsequent agreements and declarations left the status of Outer Mongolia at first sight ambiguous. Under an agreement between Russia and Mongolia in November 1912:

> The Imperial Russian Government shall assist Mongolia to maintain the autonomous regime, which she has established, as also the right to have her national army, and to admit neither the presence of Chinese troops on her territory nor the colonization of her land by the Chinese. (Article 1.)

Yet in a joint Sino-Russian declaration in November 1913, elaborated in an exchange of notes:

> I. Russia recognises that Outer Mongolia is under the suzerainty of China.
> II. China recognises the autonomy of Outer Mongolia. . . .

and the ambiguity is compounded by the exchange of notes in which it is stated:

> 1. Russia recognises that the territory of Outer Mongolia forms part of the territory of China.
> 2. As regards questions of a political and territorial nature, the Chinese Government shall come to an agreement with the Russian Government through negotiations in which the authorities of Outer Mongolia shall take part;

and the 'exact boundaries' of Outer Mongolia are to be the subject of a later conference. A tripartite agreement was concluded in June 1915 at Kyakhta, in which the 1913 Declaration and Exchange of notes was reaffirmed and,

> Article II. Outer Mongolia recognises China's suzerainty. China and Russia recognise the autonomy of Outer Mongolia forming part of Chinese territory.

A 'formal delimitation between China and autonomous Mongolia' was to be carried out by a tripartite commission. Since these texts[67] are a translation of a French text, printed in the Russian Bulletin of Laws, a text which was presumably itself a translation or a diplomatic version of Russian and Chinese terms,[68] it may be misleading to put too much weight on the language of the English text. Nevertheless the agreements are a notable illustration of the way in which conflicts of interest in a region which is a power frontier may be reduced at least for a time by the use of legal forms. On the one hand, it was accepted by Russia and the leadership of Outer Mongolia that Outer Mongolia was territorially part of China and under its suzerainty; on the other hand, China conceded that Outer Mongolia was autonomous under the rule of the Lama. Suzerainty—and the French equivalent *suzerainété*—would have described in Europe a relation between ruler and vassal based on land-holding in a feudal system; and it could be applied by analogy to the relation between the Manchu rulers and territories, such as Mongolia, inhabited by ethnically distinct peoples and placed under separate administration. As that separate administration evolved gradually into self-government for the territory, in fact or in law, it would come to be recognized as autonomous, though still part of the suzerain State. The use of the legal concepts of suzerainty and autonomy had a double advantage in these agreements. They expressed on the one hand the actual relationship between China and Outer Mongolia: in particular, autonomy set limits on Chinese intervention by sending in troops or by uncontrolled immigration ('colonization'), and it must be assumed that the Chinese administration was aware of the terms of the Russo-Mongolian agreement of 1912. On the other hand they were left sufficiently undefined to make them capable of wide interpretation in changing political circumstances. In other words, to have had no agreement would have left uncertainty of power in this border region which neither Russia nor China could tolerate, but to have cast the agreements in terms too legally precise would have set unacceptable restraints. Reduction of conflict was achieved for a time by a middle course taken within a legal framework. But the Russian revolution in 1917 led again to instability and intervention by both Russia and China, though there were no changes in the recognized boundaries.[69] In 1924 Outer Mongolia achieved independence as a republic in association with the USSR. In 1945 the US and USSR agreed at Yalta that the status quo in the Mongolian People's Republic be preserved, and its independence recognized by China after a plebiscite in October 1945 was confirmed in the Sino-Soviet Treaty of Friendship (1950). A boundary agreement was

53

concluded between China and Mongolia in December 1962, providing for some demarcation on the ground. Mongolia is now plainly within the sphere of influence of the USSR and is a member of COMECON.

On the Chinese side of the western sector of the frontier with Russia lay the region of Chinese Turkestan, later called Sinkiang and now the Xinjiang-Uigur Autonomous Province. This part of the frontier is notable not only for Russian expansion in the nineteenth century with territorial gains ranging up to a hundred miles in depth, but also for the presence of oil and gas resources. Xinjiang is also a test area for nuclear devices.

The Treaty of Peking (1860),[70] following the incorporation of the Kazakh steppes in the Russian Empire and continuing Russian movement eastwards, drew the general direction of the frontier:

> The frontier line to the west, undetermined until the present, shall follow the direction of the mountains, the courses of the great rivers and the existing line of Chinese states. Starting from the last light house called Chaburidabaga, established in 1728 . . . it runs toward the south-west as far as Lake Zaysan and from there as far as Issyk Kul or Tengri-chan . . .[71] also known as Ala Tau des Kirghises, and along these mountains as far as the possessions at Kokand.[72]

A demarcation commission was also set up, which in fact applied the principles set out in the Treaty further in the favour of Russia, the Protocol of Tarbagatai (Tahcheng) (1864) allocating to Russia territory south-east of Lake Zaysan and also the Tien-Shan region south of Issyk-Kul.

The Ili River, which rises in the eastern part of the Tien-Shan mountains, flows into Lake Balkhash, and its main valley is rich in forest, pasture land and minerals, extending from Ining (Kuldja) in Xinjiang to Ili, about 50 miles north of Alma Ata. Russia had established consulates at Ining (Kuldja) and Tarbagatai (Tahcheng), and secured other trading rights, under a treaty signed at Kuldja in 1851; but by 1800 they had moved into Kuldja and occupied a large part of the Ili valley with military force in order to protect the frontier trade. Russia appears to have given some assurance that this occupation was only temporary, but China became preoccupied with an Islamic rebellion under Yakub Beg in Dzungaria, the northern region of Xinjiang, which led to the setting up of an independent regime in Kashgar. It was not until 1878, after China had established authority in Dzungaria and the death of Yakub Beg in 1877, that China demanded Russian withdrawal from the Ili valley. Negotiations began in St. Petersburg and led to the signing of a treaty at Livadia in the Crimea in September 1879; but it was repudiated by the Manchu administration, and Chung Hau, who had been the Chinese plenipotentiary, was later put on trial. Negotiations were renewed in St. Petersburg and what was called the Treaty of Ili[73] was signed in February 1881. In substance Russia withdrew from the Kuldja area but retained a large part of the Lower Ili Valley; further, China was to pay Russia an indemnity for its occupation costs, fixed at the equivalent of nine million roubles, in fact nearly double the figure agreed in the Livadia treaty. Demarcation arrangements were also made and portions of the frontier were marked with pillars. Russia is said to have moved some boundary posts eastwards after the fall of the Manchus in 1911, but the Treaty of Ili boundaries remained stable although China has denounced the Treaty as 'unequal'. However in 1944-7 the USSR gave support to a number of attemps to secure regional autonomy by the inhabitants of northern and north-eastern Sinkiang. Clashes between Soviet and Chinese troops also took place along the northern boundary in 1969, as on the Ussuri river.

The mountainous region of the Pamirs lies in great part in the Tadzhik SSR but there has been no agreed delimitation of boundaries with China and it may be that the nature of the region, seasonally inhabited by flock-raising nomads, does not inspire territorial claims.

What light does this brief survey of the Sino-Russian frontier and its delimitation throw on the role of law?

First, it is a frontier between two empires. The present tense is still justified because, although both systems ideologically reject imperialism and colonization, they do not escape from the geopolitical structure of their territories. Here we may recall the 'salt-water fallacy', the assumption that the expansion of States overland, from the territorial core into peripheral often wholly alien lands, is somehow essentially different from that carried out overseas. The Sino-Russian frontier is in fact composed of fringe regions on both sides, many peoples of which are as distinct in language, race and culture from those living under the central power as the inhabitants of overseas territories of the UK, France or the Netherlands.

In both the Russian and Chinese systems the regions have degrees of autonomy, a political recognition of the limits to control of remote and different peoples, and it is because of this dilution of the central power as the frontier is approached that it is for both sides a region of insecurity. There are constantly possibilities of rebellion or secession, and the need to protect and exploit valuable natural resources, sometimes unexpectedly discovered.[74] The sense of insecurity will be intensified, if wider strategic needs are perceived, and both the USSR and China maintain considerable forces of armour and aircraft on both sectors of the frontier. This itself can lead to friction, if not conflict, as events on the Ussuri River and in Xinjiang in 1969 show.

What then is the influence and authority here of the law?

A bilateral agreement between States has a formal authority, because it is an accepted way of recognizing rights and undertaking obligations, the purpose of an agreement being to make policy and action on each side predictable in a given area of national interest. But as national interests change over time, so this authority may vary in practice: it may be decisive, it may have only some influence on policy, or it may be rejected. Further, its formal authority will also depend on the degree of certainty of its provisions: some may be clear and indisputable, others may be vague or open to at least two different interpretations. All these aspects of international agreements are visible in the Sino-Russian frontier agreements, as we shall shortly show.

But law had also a domestic function. Suzerainty and autonomy were in the Chinese system a delicate balance of the right of the State to govern or control its territories and the rights of certain communities to a degree of self-government or independence; further, suzerainty carried with it the principle of non-intervention by other States. Though suzerainty may no longer be used as a term, the relation it described remains in the frontier regions. The federal analogy of suzerainty has been well described by Parkinson:[75] '. . . the crucial moment in the genesis of the states-system came when certain well-placed feudal rulers succeeded in converting their fiefs—which they held on quasi-leasehold terms on condition of providing public services within the context of feudal interdependence—into unconditional freehold lands, absolving themselves in the process of all obligations towards their overlords, while retaining the feudal services of those within reach of their power.' It would not then be incorrect to describe the Tadzhik, Kirghiz and Kazakh SS Republics, though they have a constitutional right of secession, and the autonomous regions of Xinjiang-Uigur and Inner Mongolia, as being still under the suzerainty of the central power.

If we ask now what the authority of the law has been over the Sino-Russian frontier, we find that it ranges from dominance to rejection.

Contemporary China, like the USSR, strongly asserts national sovereignty, but China opposes hegemony,[76] whether of the US or USSR; and this has led both to reliance on and to rejection of the frontier treaties according to the interest being served. So the *People's Daily* (1.11.1977) was in fact reaffirming positions which China had taken for more than a century over frontier rights, and boundary agreements with Russia, when it said:[77] 'The people of every country must . . . closely watch the aggressive and expansionist activities of the two hegemonist powers and resolutely defeat them. The people must see to it that these two superpowers do not violate their country's or any other country's *sovereign rights*, do *not encroach on their country's or any other country's territory and territorial seas*, or violate their strategic areas and *strategic lines of communication*, do not use force or the threat of force or *other manoeuvres to interfere in their country's or any other country's internal affairs*; moreover, both powers must be closely watched lest they resort to schemes of subversion and use "aid" as a pretext to push through their military, political and economic plots'.

Here China is seen to be relying on the security which the certainty of boundary treaties can give, for territorial encroachment cannot be identified without delimitation of boundaries; and this certainty is recognized as necessary in the Vienna Convention on the Law of Treaties. For it states in Article 62(2) that at least:

A fundamental change of circumstances may not be invoked as a ground for terminating or withdrawing from a treaty: (a) if the treaty establishes a boundary . . .

But China has also for long kept her options open by denouncing a number of the boundary treaties with Russia as unequal, in particular the treaties of Tientsin (1850), Aigun (1858), Peking (1860) and Ili (1881). Claims for restoration of the 'traditional frontiers' began to be made after the establishment of the republic in 1912. In 1920 Karakhan, the Acting Commissar of Foreign Affairs in Russia, in a statement sponsored by Lenin, recognized the principle of unequal treaties and declared their intention 'to renounce all the previous treaties concluded with China by the Tsar, and to restore to the Chinese nation all that has been taken from it by force'. With the establishment of stable government in Russia there began the periodic negotiations over boundaries with China, which have not in half a century led to any firm and accepted realignments.

An agreement drafted in 1924 but never ratified provided that:

> The Governments of the two Contracting Parties agree to annul at the Conference[78] ... all Conventions, Treaties, Agreements, Protocols, Contracts, concluded between the Government of China and the Tsarist Government and to replace them with new treaties, agreements, etc. ... on the basis of equality, reciprocity and justice. ... (Article III)

> The Government of the USSR, in accordance with its policy and declarations of 1919 and 1920, declares that all treaties, agreements, etc., concluded between the former Tsarist Government and any third party or parties affecting the sovereign rights or interests of China are null and void. ... (Article IV)

No progress has been made since in settling the disputed boundaries. The Treaty of Friendship, Alliance and Mutual Assistance (1950) left the issues open and the USSR has certainly long abandoned the position it had taken on the boundary treaties in the negotiation of the abortive agreement of 1924. For by 1969 Foreign Minister Gromyko was saying that 'the boundaries of the Soviet Union are inviolable throughout their length', though at the same time proposing negotiations on 'certain stretches' of the frontier with China.[79] The invalidity of treaties, that may be in some ways 'unequal', was not recognized as a general principle of law in the nineteenth century and it is only since the Second World War that it has come to be formulated and accepted in international law.[80] The Vienna Convention on the Law of Treaties (1969), though not yet technically in force, may be taken to express the principle when it declares that:

> A treaty is void if its conclusion has been procured by the threat or use of force in violation of the principles of international law embodied in the Charter of the United Nations. (Article 52)

But this may be qualified by the provision for the non-retroactivity of the Vienna Convention: Article 4, and by the fact that in any case Article 52 is limited to the threat or use of force in the sense of Article 2(4) of the UN Charter. However, China would no doubt maintain not only that the principle expressed can and must be applied to some old treaties, but that the four treaties denounced by it were concluded under the pressures of territorial encroachment by

Russia using at many points military force. Support would be given to this by Article 4 itself:

> without prejudice to the application of any rules set forth in the present Convention to which treaties would be subject under international law independently of the Convention, the Convention applies only to treaties which are concluded by States after the entry into force of the present Convention with regard to such States;

and also by the Declaration annexed to the Convention in which the Conference

> solemnly condemns the threat or use of pressure in any form, whether military, political or economic, by any State to perform any act relating to the conclusion of a treaty in violation of the principles of the sovereign equality of States and freedom of consent.

Further, the 'capitulations' agreements concluded in the nineteenth century by China with Britain and France had been terminated by 1945.

But China would still be faced in law with an insoluble dilemma: either to abandon the four treaties and so treat virtually the whole of the Sino-Russian treaties as indeterminate, or to concede—contrary to the 'unequal treaty' principle—the validity of the treaty determination of the greatest part of the common boundaries, and so limit any negotiation to a few disputed areas, as proposed by the USSR. The Vienna Convention states that no separation of the provisions of a treaty is to be permitted where, in particular, Article 52 is applicable: Article 44(5).

Politically however, it is open to China to pursue both courses in turn or even at the same time, according to its perceived needs and the context; and the history of the Sino-Russian frontier to date illustrates this, and the role of law, in a number of ways. First, the law had authority, expressed in the boundary treaties to the extent that both countries had an interest in maintaining the stability in a great part of the frontier which boundary determination gave. The fact that the interpretation of the treaties may between certain points on the boundaries be disputed does not weaken the reliance of both sides on the authority of the law to support their respective claims; and this the Ussuri River Dispute in 1969 showed. Were such a dispute to be referred either to international arbitration or the

International Court of Justice, which is of course almost unimaginable, China would doubtless take the second course, pleading the certainty and permanence of boundary determination and alleging trespasses by the USSR. In any negotiation, too, on the boundaries, legal arguments would no doubt be advanced on similar lines.[81] But the first course, the appeal of China to the invalidity of 'unequal treaties' belongs to different and wider contexts: of public persuasion and of confrontation with the USSR over other issues, with which boundary determination may have no immediate connection. Here the invocation of invalidity is not in fact a legal argument at all, but the tactical use of a legal concept in a larger political strategy. Political influence, both domestic and external, is relied on rather than the authority of the law; the treaties are invoked, only to be rejected, by the same party.

China has asserted *maritime claims* in the UN Conference on the Law of the Sea, which are closely associated with seabed resources.

China has an extensive continental shelf, as defined in the Continental Shelf Convention, but Japan and the Philippines have virtually none. The Yellow Sea, the East China Sea and the Formosa Strait are all within the depth limit of 600 feet; in fact there is a depth limit of 150 feet from the Formosa Strait northward lying from 50 to 200 miles from the coast, and the average depths of the Yellow Sea and the East China Sea beyond this limit are around 200 feet. However there would in principle have to be a demarcation of the shelf in the Yellow Sea between China and Korea, which could make equal claims in that area. Continental shelf claims by Japan in the East China Sea would have to overcome the fact that from Nagasaki southwards to Taiwan there is a belt of deep water, reaching a depth of over 6,000 feet in the Okinawa Trough, which separates Japanese islands from the shelf of the East China Sea and makes it difficult to describe it as 'adjacent' to the islands. However, a similar trough lying off the west coast of Norway has not been held to deprive Norway of continental shelf rights. A line of prospective oil fields runs south through the East China Sea from Cheju Do Island to Taiwan, and near to but not within the 600 feet depth limit.

China has made territorial claims to a number of islands, which could be used as bases for maritime, including continental shelf claims, in the East China Sea. The islands claimed include of course Taiwan, and also Senkaku (Tiaoyu Tai). The Treaty of Peace and Friendship (1978) between China and Japan left the disputed sovereignty over Senkaku Islands unresolved, and made no provision for the shared or divided exploitation of the oil fields in the East China Sea.

As will be seen, when we come to consider developments in the law of the sea, the East China Sea could become an area of conflict.

Some general conclusions may also be drawn from the history of the frontiers of China on the role of law in the resolution of frontier and boundary conflicts. First, frontiers go through a certain evolution. Where distinct communities are established there will be recognition of a common frontier region dividing them geophysically or ethnically or in economic resources or development, or with a combination of these features. Then there will probably be a delimitation of the frontier by setting of boundaries in practice or by treaty provisions, followed sometimes by demarcation on the ground. There is also the continuing administration by each side of its part of the frontier region. The time element in the recognition and administration of boundaries can then be critical.

But, as the frontiers of China show, boundary treaties may be vague or ambiguous or incomplete, and there will be in any case differences both in the approach to their interpretation and its results between ministers, their diplomatic and legal advisers, and arbitral or judicial tribunals. Political and tactical consideration will guide ministers and their advisers: what use and interpretation of a boundary treaty will serve to increase power or reduce risk of conflict in the region? Can legal concepts or arguments about boundaries be of use in negotiation, either of a new boundary arrangement or of some quite different matter where one side wishes to use a boundary issue as a means of pressure? A judicial approach will be to identify precise issues, and to define the criteria by which the known facts can be organized, and binding conclusions drawn from them.

Political considerations may lead to the acceptance of a boundary, whether defined by treaty or recognized in fact, simply to avoid conflict; and this attempt to avoid conflicts has been given continental range in both Central and South America and Africa. In the former the extent of national territories, and consequently their boundaries, was to be determined by the principle *uti possidetis*, that is to say, the boundaries of the newly independent states were to follow those of the Spanish administrative units as they were in South America in 1810, and in Central America in 1821. The Organization of African Unity adopted a similar principle in 1964,[82] though Morocco and Somalia did not accept it, in a resolution of an Assembly of Heads of State and Government. The Assembly:

Considering that border problems constitute a grave and permanent factor of dissension;

Conscious of the existence of extra-African manoeuvres aimed at dividing African states;

Considering further that the borders of African States, on the day of their independence, constitute a tangible reality,

. . .

2. Solemnly declares that all Member States pledge themselves to respect the borders existing on their achievement of national independence.

But a political principle, such as *uti possidetis* or the OAU declaration, will not necessarily avoid or resolve boundary disputes, and at least one arbitral tribunal has refrained from adopting it, illustrating also the difference between the political and judicial approach. This was a Special Tribunal, established by agreement between Guatemala and Honduras to determine the boundary line between them, it being declared that 'the only line that can be established *de jure* between their respective countries is that of the *uti possidetis* of 1821': Article V; however the Tribunal was authorized to take account of 'interests' acquired by either side across the boundary during its later development. The Tribunal in its Award[83] did not on the one hand question the political efficacy of a boundary recognized by both sides in their administrative practice; so with regard to the *uti possidetis* principle:

The Constitutions of the new States, and the governmental acts of each, especially when unopposed or when initial opposition was not continued, are of special importance.

On the other hand, the Tribunal noted:

. . . particular difficulties in drawing the line of '*uti possidetis* of 1821', by reason of the lack of trustworthy information during colonial times with respect to a large part of the territory in dispute. Much of this territory other parts of which had occasionally been visited were but vaguely known.

Nevertheless the Tribunal asserted its duty to provide a definitive settlement:

In the light of the declared purpose of the Treaty [establishing the Tribunal], the Tribunal is not at liberty to conclude that the lack of adequate evidence to establish the line of *uti possidetis* of 1821, throughout the entire territory in dispute, relieves the Tribunal of the duty to determine the definitive boundary to its full extent . . . to the end that the question of territorial boundaries may be finally and amicably settled.

The objective of friendly settlement, which can characterize arbitral as distinct from judicial procedure, does not alter here the judicial criteria adopted.

The conclusions to be drawn are perhaps that the historical record, particularly the more remote it is in time, may be of little help and even irrelevant to the contemporary application of international rules and standards; and that the intertemporal rule must in fact be applied in reverse, so that international relations are not seen as governed by obsolescent concepts.

Power-frontier confrontations: Berlin (1948–58) and Cuba (1962)

A number of power-frontier confrontations have arisen since 1945: in Korea (1945–50), Berlin (1948), Suez (1956), Cuba (1962), Vietnam (1965–9), and Afghanistan (1980). Illustrations can be found among them of enduring power frontiers, which may be for long periods quiescent but in which sharp and clear conflicts can arise from time to time; of the emergence of collective intervention, particularly by the UN; and of the role of law as a factor in the behaviour of States and organizations concerned.

Much has been written about them,[84] and it would serve no purpose to describe them in detail here. What will be attempted is the identification of the kinds of conflict they represent, an account of the forms of intervention 'across the frontier' that constituted the conflict, and an assessment of the role of law.

Conflicts on a power frontier, as we have described it earlier, may be critical, where a major shift or even elimination of the frontier itself is likely to take place as the result of action from one side; the conflict may be of a second order, where the frontier is being disturbed or weakened. Conflicts may also be central, in that there is a direct confrontation of countries on each side of the power frontier, or peripheral, where the frontier serves to protect distant areas of strategic or resource interest to a particular country.

The conflicts chosen for consideration also reflect features of contemporary international relations, which are to a great extent new since 1945. First, while the US and USSR are still seen in some contexts as the great bipolarity, the alliance of the countries of

Western Europe—former enemies—the rise of China, and the emergence of OPEC, have together made the world multipolar at the higher levels of power and influence. Further, the 'Group of 77', numbering now perhaps 120, is a medium for the exercise of political influence by the smaller or poorer countries in international relations, which may be still far from decisive, but was earlier unknown. Secondly, as a consequence in part of these changes and in part of the slow spread of nuclear weapons, there has been a reduction of power differentials, at least where conflicts came close to the use of armed force. There is a greater hesitation to exert power by the use of force in international relations. As Lord Mountbatten observed:[85] 'The nuclear arms race has no military purpose. Wars cannot be fought with nuclear weapons. Their existence only adds to our perils.' Thirdly, the domestic order of countries, while never wholly ignored in international relations, has become a prime factor. Political activists seen and then praised or condemned as liberals or nationalists or Marxists or freedom-fighters according to the angle of view, are rendering many countries unstable; and civil conflicts in those that lie on power frontiers inevitably attract intervention. Much turns on the difficulties, on the one hand, which the ruling groups in 'third world' countries have in meeting demands for political participation from ethnic communities, and middle- and working-class groups, farming with improved methods of production and even slow economic growth; and on the other hand on the fears generated at the higher levels of power by political instability or overturns in countries along a power frontier.[86]

The Berlin conflict was both critical and central. The Soviet blockade of Berlin, consisting finally of denial of access by road, rail or canal of Western forces or supplies, commenced in June 1948 and was complete by early August. Extended talks achieved no results, and the Security Council, to which the issue was referred in September 1948, declared itself competent despite Soviet objections to discuss it but found no solution; in particular, a proposal that it be referred to a committee of experts was rejected. However, the success of the airlift of needed supplies to the Western sectors of Berlin, which began in August 1948 and was organized in a Combined Airlift Task Force in October, was doubtless decisive in persuading the USSR to moderate its policy. Secret negotiations between the US and USSR representatives in the Security Council, following talks in Berlin and Moscow including a pronouncement by Stalin, led to the termination of the blockade in May 1949. The establishment of the Federal Republic of Germany and the German Democratic Republic followed rapidly in the same year.

In the earlier stages of the Zonal occupation of Germany the USSR had urged the conclusion of a peace treaty with a single Germany. But this idea was not pursued and as relations between the Allied Powers deteriorated, the line of division between the Eastern and Western zones of occupation became a visible power frontier. The special position of Berlin made it the point of balance on this frontier. The blockade was imposed ostensibly because of the proposed currency reform in West Germany and introduction of the new D-Mark into West Berlin. The blockade raised a conflict, which was critical in that the denial of access to Berlin of the Western powers was a challenge both to their governmental authority, and their status in relation to Germany, which they could not accept without major political and strategic disadvantage. The conflict was also central in that there was a direct confrontation between the civil authorities and the military forces of the USSR and the Western powers. Their decision to hold on in Berlin, and bring in supplies by air, was described by Foreign Secretary Ernest Bevin in these words: 'His Majesty's Government and our Western Allies can see no alternative between that and surrender, and none of us can accept surrender.'

The conflict created by Soviet demands concerning Berlin in 1958, as it developed in the following years with the building of the Berlin wall in August 1961 was, in comparison with that of 1948, of a second order. Coral Bell has aptly described the various actions taken as a transformation from *source* of crisis to *symbol* of crisis;[87] and the Berlin wall, though it had a practical purpose of reducing the westward flow through Berlin of emigrants from the German Democratic Republic, was and is still a symbol of the power frontier.

The role of law is plain. In the first place, the right of access to the city was the subject of the crisis in 1948, though not the cause of conflict in the broader sense between the Allied Powers. It was not expressly set out in any written agreement, but was necessarily implied in the agreement, reached in November 1944, that the Allied Powers would govern Germany jointly through the Allied Control Council, and in the division of Berlin into administrative sectors between them. The right of access was also recognized in practice, in the initial arrangement for access to Berlin from the West by railway from Magdeburg, by *autobahn* from Helmstedt, and through two air corridors, increased to three in November 1945; the use of these

C

means of access did not depend on advance notice. There was, then, a legal right of access, and this was not in fact formally denied by the USSR.[88]

However, the enforceability of the right depended on how far each side was prepared to go in the use of force; for example, by interference with the airlift by the USSR or military action on road and rail by the Western powers. In fact, the intermediate recourse to the Security Council was taken. France, UK and US sent identical notes to the UN Secretary General on 29.9.1948, bringing to the attention of the Security Council the threat to the peace which, they asserted, had been created by the measures of blockade.

The USSR advanced tactical legal arguments to the effect that the Security Council was not competent to deal with the matter in view of Article 107 of the UN Charter, which provides that:

> Nothing in the present Charter shall invalidate or preclude action, in relation to any State which during the Second World War has been an enemy of any signatory to the present Charter, taken or authorised as a result of that war by the Governments having responsibility for such action.

In particular, it argued that various international agreements relating to Germany, including those concluded at Yalta and Potsdam, bound the Four Powers to refer matters concerning them to the Council of Foreign Ministers, and that the three Western powers were in breach of these agreements in bringing the Berlin blockade to the Security Council; it maintained that in any case Article 107 placed action taken in respect of Berlin outside the UN Charter and that the Security Council was therefore not competent to deal with it.

In the debate that followed, the Council analysed Article 107 at length, some fine points of interpretation being made. Perhaps decisive in its rejection of the USSR arguments were first, that the duties of the Security Council in the maintenance of international peace and security, laid down in Article 24 without qualification, overrode any limitation in Article 107; and, secondly, that in any case the opening words of Article 107 dealt only with the consistency with the Charter of action taken and not with the competence of UN organs to consider that consistency, and further that action taken in respect of Berlin could only be covered by Article 107 if taken by the governments responsible, that is, the Four Powers in occupation of Germany at that time.

It can be said, then, that the Berlin power frontier had a legal framework, clearly defined, which set limits to action taken, singly or jointly, by the Four Powers, and which was regarded by all of them as essential to the stability of the power frontier, a fact illustrated by the abandonment of the blockade and by the maintenance of the Berlin regime in the Quadripartite Agreement (1972). In imposing the blockade, the USSR went outside the limits set and so was in breach of the relevant agreements. But there was no sanction either consequential or immediately available as a constraint, and recourse to the Security Council failed, though it is to be noted that negotiation was conducted in its final stages in the Security Council forum between the US and USSR representatives. However, the blockade was in fact terminated.

The Berlin crisis in 1948 illustrates three features of the role of law in international relations: that a legal regime may be established and recognized to secure the stability of a power frontier; that its rules may be broken for various ulterior motives, and such breaches and objections to them may be subject to tactical legal arguments; and that observance of the law can depend in the end not on external constraints but on the need to secure certain shared objectives, such as stability of the power frontier.

The introduction of arms[89] by the USSR into Cuba, with the full cooperation of its government, in July and August 1962, brought the USSR into central and critical conflict with the US. It was a strong military intrusion into an area so close to the United States that its power frontier could be seen as eliminated there, given the range and capacity of the missiles. It was central in that the operation brought the US and USSR into direct confrontation.

In the evolution of this short and sharp crisis, the influence of law was almost wholly limited to the choice of response by the US to the intervention in Cuba by the USSR, and to the form given to that response. Whether the introduction of the missiles and other instruments of war was itself unlawful was little debated. As far as its western hemisphere treaty obligations went, Cuba had repudiated the Inter-American Treaty of Mutual Assistance (1947)—the Rio Treaty —in September 1960 and had been excluded from participation in the organs of the Organization of American States in January 1962. Further, given the Bay of Pigs invasion of Cuba by emigré forces in April 1961, in which some operational participation by the United States was not disputed, it was open to Cuba to invoke the principle of anticipatory self-defence, under Article 51 of the UN Charter, against a possible second armed attack, to justify the emplacement of the missiles. But, while these considerations might legitimize the admission of the missiles by Cuba, they would not necessarily cover the position of the USSR. For here it might be said that the MRBM and IRBM went beyond the requirements of self-defence of Cuba against another invasion, and were offensive weapons directed against the US as part of USSR strategy; this could constitute a threat of force contrary to Article 2(4) of the UN Charter.

However, none of these considerations appear to have been pressed, and President Kennedy clearly avoided legal issues in his denunciation of the USSR. He cast it rather in power-frontier terms on the one hand, calling the action a 'deliberately provocative and unjustified change in the status quo', and warning the USSR that any western hemisphere use of the missiles would meet a 'full retaliatory response against the Soviet Union'; on the other hand, it was a 'clandestine, reckless and provocative threat to world peace', calling for Security Council intervention. Nor did the US invoke or rely upon the Monroe doctrine in its historic form, a principal reason being that it would not have the support of at least some OAS members. As President Wilson had observed: 'The Monroe doctrine was proclaimed by the United States on her own authority. It always has been maintained, and always will be maintained, upon her own responsibility.'

Further, its principles had been reshaped in the post-1945 moves towards community in the Americas. President Monroe had said: 'The American continents, by the free and independent condition which they have assumed, are henceforth not to be considered as subjects for future colonization by any European powers. . . .' and 'The political system of the allied powers is essentially different . . . from that of America. . . . We should consider any attempt on their part to extend their system to any portion of this hemisphere as dangerous to our peace and safety.' But, although these principles were not wholly inapposite to the situation in Cuba in 1962, they were virtually reformulated in the OAS Charter, Article 28 of which provides:

> If the inviolability or the integrity of the territory or the sovereignty of political independence or any American State should be affected by . . . an act of aggression which is not an armed attack or by an extracontinental conflict . . . or by any other fact or situation that might endanger the peace of America, the American States, in furtherance of the principles of hemispheric solidarity or

collective self-defence, shall apply the measures and procedures established in the special treaties on the subject.

A prime treaty is the Rio Treaty, Article 6 of which, contemplating identical circumstances to those described in Article 28 of the OAS Charter, requires the Organ of Consultation to meet immediately to decide on the measures to be taken for the maintenance of the peace and security of the Continent; Article 8 describes these measures, ranging from the breaking of diplomatic relations to the use of armed force, similar to those in Articles 41 and 42 of the UN Charter.

These provisions, while setting some limit to US action, also broadened the possibility of support for it. On the one hand, an obligation on the US as a member State not to take wholly independent action in such circumstances is implied; and the missile crisis could be seen as such a circumstance. On the other hand, both the OAS and Security Council were in a position to give at least political support to US action. The US had, then, recourse to both bodies.

The OAS Council, constituting itself an Organ of Consultation under the Rio Treaty, passed a virtually unanimous resolution (19–0–1) calling for the withdrawal of the missiles from Cuba and recommending that member States:

> ... take all measures individually and collectively including the use of armed force which they deem necessary to assure that the Government of Cuba cannot continue to receive from the Sino-Soviet powers military material and related supplies which may threaten the peace and security of the Continent ...

However, though directed to the 'defensive quarantine' established by the US in relation to shipments of 'offensive weapons' to Cuba, and implying approval of it, this Resolution could not be said to authorize or legitimize it. Article 53(1) of the UN Charter prohibits enforcement action under regional arrangements 'without the authorization of the Security Council', except under Article 107, not applicable here. Given the terms of the Presidential Order,[90] and the reference to the use of armed force in the Resolution itself, the quarantine must have been regarded as a form of enforcement action; but it could not, since the Security Council made no decision authorizing it or indeed any decision on the matter, itself authorize it as a regional arrangement.[91] The legality of the quarantine remains then in question, at least under the High Seas Convention, which was ratified by the US in 1961 and came into force a few weeks before the establishment of the quarantine, and particularly Articles 9 or 22.[92] Even if it were to be regarded as a pacific blockade—a description noticeably avoided at the time—these provisions would restrict or even preclude it.

It may then be said that the issues in the Cuban missile crisis were neither defined nor resolved by law. It was not the lawfulness of the introduction of missiles into Cuba by the USSR that was challenged but their strategic threat; and the conformity of the quarantine with international law was not certain or determined. The choice of responses by the US was dictated primarily by the need to avoid action that could intensify the conflict,[93] and the desirability of obtaining support both domestic[94] and within the OAS, for the action taken. But there were still legal elements here: on the one hand, an airstrike against Cuba, though indicated by some, was rejected not least because it would have been legally hard to defend; on the other hand, the recourse to the OAS Council and Security Council was also a fulfilment of a duty under the respective Charters, and the quarantine itself could be seen as an effort to maintain peace by the least use of force and giving an opportunity to the adversary to withdraw. It was perhaps after all a corollary of the Monroe doctrine, enunciated by President Theodore Roosevelt in 1904: '... in the Western Hemisphere the adherence of the United States to the Monroe doctrine may force the United States, however reluctantly, in flagrant cases of ... wrong-doing or impotence, to the exercise of an international police power.'

Control of intervention: Suez (1956) and Afghanistan (1980)

Direct intervention 'across the frontier' was avoided in the Berlin confrontation, and the indirect intervention of the USSR in Cuba was effectively withdrawn. However, two of the confrontations mentioned—Suez (1956) and Afghanistan (1980)—arose over direct interventions. How far were they controlled and to what extent by law?

It may be said that the Suez Canal was the focal intersection of two power frontiers, the one running more or less from north to south from Turkey to the Sudan, and the other running notionally from east to west. The first was the frontier of the Middle East, where lie vital economic resources, and which the Axis powers endeavoured to penetrate in the North African campaign of the Second World War. It was secured in older times by the British control of Cyprus, the line of Mandates, the Anglo-Egyptian base agreements, and the Anglo-Egyptian Protectorate over the Sudan. The second frontier was in effect the Canal itself, as the gate leading to the Indian Ocean from Western Europe, and seen as having prime economic and strategic importance.

In the Suez Canal in 1956 the elements of confrontation were wide-ranging, some going far back; and it could be described as both central and critical. If, at the risk of some distortion, we limit these elements to those occurring from July to November 1956, five stand out: the political reaction of the UK, with which France was associated; the confrontation between Israel and Egypt; the 'nationalization' of the Suez Canal Company; the armed intervention in Egypt; and the opposition of the US, supported in the UN, to British, French and Israeli action against Egypt.

In the UK the 'nationalization' of the Suez Canal Company by the Egyptian Decree of 26 July 1956 was seen not only as bringing the use and operation of the Canal out of international, under the 1888 Convention, and into Egyptian control; but also as a symbolic act of Arab nationalist power, comparable to the occupation of the Rhineland under Hitler. The virtual unanimity of the political leadership of the UK that vital interests and assets, particularly in oil resources, were imperilled, is shown by the statement in Parliament of Hugh Gaitskell, then leader of the opposition:[95] 'We cannot forget that Colonel Nasser has repeatedly boasted of his intention to create an Arab empire from the Atlantic to the Persian Gulf. . . . If Colonel Nasser's prestige is put up sufficiently and ours is put down, effects of that in that part of the world will be that our friends desert us because they think we are lost, and go over to Egypt. . . . It is all very familiar. It is exactly the same as we encountered from Mussolini and Hitler in those years before the war.' Prime Minister Eden, with his Cabinet and Chiefs of Staff, were agreed that 'the Canal is an international asset and facility, which is vital to the free world', that economic pressures on Egypt would be unlikely to be effective, and that 'we must be ready in the last resort, to use force to bring Nasser to his senses.' Further, it was necessary not to get involved in 'legal quibbles about the rights of the Egyptian Government to nationalize what is technically an Egyptian company'.[96]

In these statements the Suez Canal was plainly seen as a power frontier in two ways; it was a crucial part in a line of growing Arab nationalism, which could set new limits to Western interests and influence; and it was a small, but for Western powers vital, passage to and from strategic areas, including sources of oil.

The confrontation between Israel and Egypt needs little elaboration. There were the continuing Egyptian restrictions, at least legally questionable under the 1888 Convention, on passage through the Canal of Israeli ships and Israel-bound cargoes; the *fedayeen* raids on Israel, and punitive reprisals such as the Israeli counter-attack on the Gaza Strip in February 1956; and the corresponding increase in Egyptian armaments, supplied in great part from Eastern Europe.

The 'nationalization' of the Suez Canal Company by Egypt, and its possible consequences for the use and management of the Canal, was also of concern to a large number of countries, whose vessels were in constant transit through it; and there was little difficulty in assembling an international conference in London in August 1956 to consider the issues. Two approaches were suggested, both based upon a continued international regime: the USSR, Ceylon, India and Indonesia together proposed the establishment of an international advisory regime, but the great majority sought full international control of the Canal, while recognizing the territorial sovereignty of Egypt. The Egyptian rejection of these proposals led to the formation of a Suez Canal Users Association at the beginning of October. The armed intervention in Egypt, doubtless collusive, began with the invasion by Israel of the Sinai Peninsula on 29 October 1956. On the next day the UK and France called for a cease-fire, for a withdrawal of both Israeli and Egyptian forces to 10 miles from the Canal, for Egypt to accept the temporary stationing of Anglo-French forces in the Canal Zone, and for acceptance of these various terms within 12 hours. Egypt rejected them. UK aircraft carried out bombing raids along the Canal on 31 October and on 5 November paratroops were landed, and Port Said was bombarded from the sea and occupied.

Finally, there were major political differences between the US on the one hand and the UK and France on the other on how the situation should be handled. The US was determined to bring about a peaceful settlement of the dispute within the framework of the UN Charter. It resolutely opposed the use of force, introduced the Security Council resolution on 30 October, the day after Israel invaded Sinai, calling on Israel to withdraw and upon the UK and France to 'refrain from force', and refused any monetary support to the UK, when sterling came under heavy pressure, this last measure of disassociation being probably decisive.

Undisputed was the regime established by the first two clauses of the Suez Canal Convention (1888) Article 1:

> The Suez Maritime Canal shall always be free and open, in time of war as in time of peace, to every vessel of commerce or war, without distinction of flag. Consequently the High Contracting Parties agree not in any way to interfere with the free use of the Canal, in time of war as in time of peace.

This legal regime was the ground upon which the principal Canal users, and particularly the United Kingdom and France, were standing; and President Nasser declared repeatedly that the Convention remained in force, and that Egypt continued to be bound by it. But of the other legal factors in the causes and handling of the crisis, there were few that were not disputed or ignored or left unresolved in effect. They entered principally in the status and 'nationalization' of the Suez Canal Company; the Egyptian restrictions on Israeli traffic through the Canal; and the justification for armed intervention advanced by Israel and by the UK and France respectively.

The status of the Compagnie Universelle du Canal Maritime de Suez, operating under concessions granted in 1854 and 1856, modified by subsequent agreements concluded by Egypt, was not obvious; much depended on whether the form of incorporation, the structure, or the assigned functions of the Company were regarded as determinative. Here the concepts have changed over the last century. R. R. Baxter has well said: 'An enterprise which would in a modern world be undertaken only by a governmental agency or by an international organization was in the mid-nineteenth century characteristically left to private initiative.'[97] The Suez Canal Company had its *siège social* in Alexandria, but its *domicile administratif* in Paris, which was its 'domicile légal et attributif de juridiction'; the British Government owned 44 per cent of the shares after 1875; and the Conseil d'Administration was composed of 32 members representing the principal countries concerned in the enterprise.[98] The Concession of 1866, modifying some of the terms of the earlier concessions affirmed the Egyptian status of the Company, but also its subordination for certain purposes to French law, thus marking the legal ambiguities:

> La Compagnie Universelle du Canal Maritime de Suez étant Egyptienne, elle est règie par les lois et usages du pays, toutefois en ce qui regarde sa constitution comme Société et les rapports des

associés entre eux, elle est, par une convention spéciale, réglée
par les lois qui en France régissent les Société anonymes. . . .
(Article 16)

The essential provisions of the Egyptian law No. 285 (26.7.1956)
'nationalizing' the Company were that 'All its funds and rights and
obligations connected therewith are transferred to the State. All
bodies and committees at present existing for its administration are
dissolved' (Article I). Compensation for shareholders and holders of
foundation bonds was prescribed and 'An independent body shall
undertake the management of the traffic in the Suez Canal' (Article
II), this body to be 'attached to the Ministry of Commerce', and to
retain 'all the present officials, employees and workmen of the
nationalized company' (Article IV). Whatever might have been the
conclusions of an arbitral or judicial tribunal on the validity and
effects of this legislation, it was doubtless the fact that under Articles
II and IV the administration of the Canal was placed in Egyptian
hands, which governed the reaction of the principal Canal users.
Prime Minister Eden had urged the avoidance of 'legal quibbles' and
firmly described the Company as an 'international organization'. The
decision then to raise political and not legal objections indirectly
conceded the validity of the Nationalization Law and left the
interested countries to seek only a substitute international regime
in place of the defunct Company.

The legal status of the Egyptian restrictions on Israel-bound traffic
in the Canal was also, perhaps surprisingly, given little attention by
the UK and France. It could be asked whether the restrictions could
really be justified as measures of the 'defence of Egypt' against
Israel under Article X of the Suez Canal Convention,[99] given other
provisions and in particular Article I, quoted above; or as an
exercise of the 'inherent right of . . . self-defence' under Article 51 of
the UN Charter. The Security Council had rejected both arguments,
the first by implication and the second expressly, in its Resolution in
1951 calling for a withdrawal of the restrictions. It also found them
to be inconsistent with the Armistice Agreement. However, Egypt
maintained the restrictions and no further action was taken by the
Security Council in regard to the Canal for the next five years.

To make some public defence of its armed intervention in Egypt,
the UK Government introduced some amateurish legal considerations. In the House of Commons it declared that:

In the present international system, where the Security Council is subject to the veto, there must be the right for individual countries to intervene in an emergency to take action to defend their own nationals and their own interests

and that, in any case, the Security Council 'cannot act immediately'. The right of self-defence in Article 51 of the Charter was also invoked by the Government to meet 'an imminent threat to our nationals', as was the British reservation of 'vital interests' in the Pact of Paris (1928). Not surprisingly, this factitious reasoning convinced nobody. The inability of the Security Council to act immediately was both obvious and irrelevant, when the UK and France, planning to use force, themselves vetoed the Resolution (30.10.1956) calling on them to refrain. Intervention in force to protect nationals, even if it was not excluded by Article 2(4) of the UN Charter, could not be justified unless there was a manifest threat to nationals, and an inability or failure of the foreign authorities to protect them, and a strict confinement of intervention to actual means of protecting them. This combination of conditions was not met by the Anglo-French intervention. The appeal to 'vital interests' would also have been more plausible had by this been meant the interests of the Canal users as a whole, infringed in fact by the Egyptian blockade of Israeli ships and cargoes, and potentially by the Egyptian take-over of the administration of the Canal. This was hinted at in a subsequent Government statement in the House of Lords (10.12.1956):

... it was essentially a case for immediate police action ... to bring the war to an end and to protect the free passage of the Canal from the hazards of that war.

But that still does not touch the heart of the conflict, Egyptian control of the Canal. The General Assembly, taking over from the Security Council, deadlocked by the vetoes, adopted a US resolution on 2 November, calling for an immediate cease-fire and withdrawal of forces, by a massive majority of 64–5 (Australia, France, Israel, New Zealand, UK). The General Assembly then proceeded to establish the UN Emergency Force.

To summarize the function of law in the Suez Canal crisis:

the international regime of the Suez Canal, and in particular the rules governing its use, not only determined much of the action but as a whole survived, though the breach of the rules was not stopped;

75

the management of the Canal was given a more national legal structure, national incorporation being combined with defined international powers and duties;

the Anglo-French intervention was controlled and terminated under UN Charter rules;

tactical legal arguments were used to defend the intervention, which were if anything counter-productive, and show that in international relations bad law can make hard cases.

The economic coercion exercised by Arab countries against Israel, of which the long-maintained closure of the Suez Canal by Egypt to Israeli or Israel-bound shipping was a part, is also an example of collective intervention, which has in fact neither on the one hand achieved its object nor on the other been brought under international control. The prime object has been to compel Israel to end its occupation of territories, taken by it in June 1967, and to secure self-determination for the Palestinian people, whether as refugees or as inhabitants of formerly Palestinian territory and in particular the West Bank, which is subject to a policy of Israeli settlement.

The legal claims with respect to former Palestinian territory made by Israel and Jordan, and on behalf of the Palestinian people, now led by the Palestine Liberation Organization (PLO), have been in continuing conflict since 1948 and have not been resolved either judicially or by conclusion of agreements. The West Bank remains the centre of conflict partly because its population is around 600,000 and almost wholly Arab, with an estimated number of 160,000 Arab refugees seeking to return to it, and partly because of the long-term policy of Israeli settlement. It is reported that there are 32 settlements in the Jordan rift area and 30 settlements in the West Bank highlands, the settlements having an average population of 8,000–10,000.[100] The attitude of Arab countries to PLO claims is strikingly shown in their rejection of a claim even by Jordan to annex the West Bank in April 1950. The Annexation Decree §. 2 had declared that:

Arab rights in Palestine shall be protected. These rights shall be defended by all possible legal means, and this unity shall in no way be connected with the final settlement of Palestine's just cause within the limits of national hopes, Arab cooperation and international justice.

76

But the Arab League found this purported annexation to be contrary to its Resolution adopted in April 1948, which stated that the entry of Arab military forces into Palestine was to be regarded as 'temporary and devoid of any character of the occupation or partition of Palestine', which was after 'liberation' to be 'handed over to its owners to rule in the way they like'.

The United Nations, which had designed without success political and territorial regimes for Palestine and Jerusalem after the termination of the Mandate in 1948 maintained the line after the war of 1967 that only a policy of cooperation between the neighbouring countries could in the long run resolve the Middle East conflicts. The General Assembly and the Security Council did not then seek to determine the specific legal issues—the rights of belligerent occupants, historic claims to territory, the limits of self-defence—but to try to lead the way to political settlement.

So the General Assembly, in Resolution 2253-ESV adopted on 4.7.1967, declared the unification of Jerusalem by Israeli occupation to be invalid and called on Israel 'to rescind all measures already taken and to desist forthwith from taking any action which would alter the status of Jerusalem'. On 22.11.1967 the Security Council adopted the comprehensive Resolution 242 unanimously, which contained the essential elements of a political settlement:

Resolution 242 states that:

THE SECURITY COUNCIL,

Expressing its continuing concern with the grave situation in the Middle East,

Emphasizing the inadmissibility of the acquisition of territory by war and the need to work for a just and lasting peace in which every State in the area can live in security,

Emphasizing further that all Member States in their acceptance of the Charter of the United Nations have undertaken a commitment to act in accordance with Article 2 of the Charter.

1. Affirms that the fulfilment of Charter principles requires the establishment of a just and lasting peace in the Middle East which should include the application of both the following principles:

(i) Withdrawal of Israeli armed forces from territories occupied in the recent conflict:

(ii) Termination of all claims or states of belligerency and re-

77

spect for and acknowledgement of the sovereignty, territorial integrity and political independence of every State in the
area and their right to live in peace within secure and
recognized boundaries free from threats or acts of force;

2. Affirms further the necessity

(a) For guaranteeing freedom of navigation through international waterways in the area;

(b) For achieving a just settlement of the refugee problem;

(c) For guaranteeing the territorial inviolability and political
independence of every State in the area, through measures
including the establishment of demilitarized zones. . . .

Neither Resolution has been effectively implemented. Nevertheless
Resolution 242 lays down, within the framework of non-use of force,
the elemental conditions of a political settlement—withdrawal of
Israeli military government from the occupied territories, the recognition and accommodation of the claims of the Palestinian people,
and the demilitarization of at least some of the frontiers once
boundary lines have been established. Further, the UN Truce Commission Organization (UNTSO), established in 1948 in association
with the Truce Commission appointed by the Security Council, performed an enduring and valuable function as observer in critical
areas and as a consequent source of information to the UN. Rosalyn
Higgins has noted that: 'Whether or not Israeli consent was legally
required for the stationing of United Nations observers on the
eastern side of the Canal [after the 'Six day war' in 1967], it was obviously essential politically that it be obtained. Both Egypt and
Israel gave their consent.'[101] But UNTSO was not able to prevent the outbreak of new hostilities in the 'Yom Kippur war' of
October 1973; and in response the Arab countries had further recourse to economic coercion directed against assumed allies of
Israel, but also linked with a change in oil-price policy. A selective
embargo on oil exports was introduced by OPEC, the embargo being
total against the US and the Netherlands; and the price of oil was
increased, in line with an earlier OPEC decision, that of Persian Gulf
crude oil rising from $2·30 to $11·65 per barrel between October
1973 and January 1974. Further, the main element in the Arab boycott of trade with foreign firms having subsidiary companies or
plants in Israel was the deprivation of Israel of oil brought in by
pipe-line.

Collective intervention by a group of countries by economic

coercion is not then obviously effective at least where the target-country has useful allies or has itself substantial economic resources. Symbolic action to influence or coerce a target-country has even less authority.

The armed intervention of the USSR in Afghanistan towards the end of 1979 can illustrate both. Like the Suez intervention in 1956, it led to wide international protest, led by the US. It is of interest that, as in the Cuba missile crisis in 1962, the US in its public declarations did not raise legal issues over the intervention in Afghanistan, perhaps because there were some similarities between it and the US intervention in force in the Dominican Republic in April 1965. Further, if it were to be said that the Soviet intervention was contrary to Article 2(4) of the UN Charter, it could be asked whether it was nevertheless justifiable in part as a measure of protection of USSR nationals, given the storming of the Soviet Embassy and murder of six of its staff in October 1979 and in part on the ground that it was with the consent of the Babrak Karmal regime, which took power in fact shortly after the intervention, based on the USSR-Afghanistan Treaty (5.12.1978), which had provided in particular for maintenance of mutual 'territorial integrity and independence', and 'cooperation' in the military field. As regards the first ground, the US appears to consider that the ill-treatment of diplomats can justify international intervention, including the use of force.

But, any legal elements in the situation being left aside as inconclusive, the political impact of such economic embargoes as are available against the USSR, and of purely symbolic action, such as withdrawals from the Olympic games, are visibly too slight to alter or reverse action seen by the other side as a necessary precautionary measure.

3 Economic Power

The exercise of economic power in international relations may more directly serve prime national interests such as economic growth and the access to resources. But there have over the past century been increasing changes both in the scale and the balance of economic power. The vast expansion of capital investment, at home and abroad, led, through the sale or loan of capital equipment, the acquisition of land and plantations, and commercial banking, to accumulations of capital and of assets in foreign territories. These were largely in private hands in the advanced countries, and protected by widespread colonial rule. But these countries also became progressively dependent on import of raw materials from an outer circle of primary producers, for the most part poor and backward countries; further, from 1945 other factors have also contributed to a different relation of economic power between the industrialized countries and the less developed countries, as they have come to be called: demands for development recognized in the formation of the IBRD, and consequent increase in international indebtedness; the moves to independence, far quicker than predicted, of the still non-self-governing territories; great government intervention in most countries in economic policy and management; and concern over the exhaustibility of natural resources. All these have been factors in widening conflicts between the industrialized countries and the less developed countries, and some principles, not always mutually compatible, have come to be asserted to resolve these conflicts by limitation of economic power.

Protection of investment

The UN General Assembly, as a world forum composed of transient political *blocs*, of which the 'Group of 77' has been influential in economic fields, has endeavoured to formulate these principles in a series of Resolutions, culminating in the Charter of Economic Rights and Duties of States,[102] already mentioned above. It can be fairly described as in great part an assertion of the claims of the less developed countries, and the negative votes and abstentions of the industrialized countries are not then surprising, particularly with regard to Articles 1 and 2, which are central. Article 1 says that a State has full and permanent sovereignty over its wealth and resources, including their use and disposal, implying there is a right of their expropriation, even when in the hands of foreign investors and developers. This principle was also stated in the Lima Declaration (1975) adopted by 82–1 (US)–7, affirming the 'inalienable right of any State to exercise freely its sovereignty and permanent control over its natural resources . . . including the right of nationalization'. Of the European Communities, France and the Netherlands expressly opposed this clause, though supporting the Declaration as a whole, along with Ireland and Denmark. The other members abstained, except Luxembourg which was not represented. Article 2 deals with expropriation, though confusing several different ideas in speaking of the right 'to nationalize, expropriate, transfer ownership of foreign property'. Normally expropriation would mean a transfer of ownership, while nationalization may comprise transfer of ownership of assets, including shares, or establishment of control, for example, by majority shareholding or participation in management. Article 2 declares that the regulation and control of foreign investments, and the expropriation or other nationalization of foreign property, shall be, in the absence of special agreement, exclusively matters of domestic law and policy. In short, international law, still invoked in earlier General Assembly Resolutions, is excluded. Belgium, Denmark, the Federal Republic of Germany, Luxembourg, UK and US voted against the Resolution as a whole, and Japan voted against Article 2. The vote in Article 2(2)c was 104–16–6.

Does the law still give any support to the opposition to these provisions of the Charter? It is argued of course that the Charter is only a General Assembly Resolution, and therefore its provisions can rank no higher than recommendations. Not only then do they not in every sense establish rules or *make* law, but they cannot be even said to have *declared* what the law is, given the dissent of most of the industrialized countries, whose voices must have decisive force on major issues of international economic policy. Here statements by some less-developed countries, made in connection with their vote for the adoption of the Charter, are said[103] to indicate reservations about the meaning and effect of Article 2: for example, Indonesia indicated that it 'would fully respect the obligations in bilateral or multilateral agreements on foreign investment, in which the question of nationalization and compensation was clearly stated'. Iran stated that Article 2 was understood by it 'as being without prejudice to any arrangements or agreements reached between States concerning investments and the modalities of compensation in the event of nationalization or expropriation of foreign property'. Jordan declared that 'while it was the sovereign right of every State to nationalize foreign property if legitimate circumstances so required, the rights of foreign investors should be adequately guaranteed in accordance with international law and in the interest of international co-operation'. Thailand 'will continue to respect international agreements and the rules of international law'. These statements at least are hardly convincing, since only Jordan makes no express mention of special agreements, and even its reference to international law could be understood as no more than pointing to the legal obligations imposed by such agreements.

It is also of interest that the International Economic, Social and Cultural Rights Covenant (1976) not only makes no specific reference to property rights, and in particular does not prohibit their 'arbitrary deprivation' as does the Universal Declaration of Human Rights (1948), but purports to grant developing countries a remarkable privilege. It would allow a developing country to deny the economic rights, set out in the Covenant, to non-nationals, having due regard to human rights, whatever that qualification may mean. Further, the rejection by Libya of the Oil Arbitration award,[104] and by Argentina of the Beagle Channel Arbitration award,[105] suggest that the provisions of Article 2 of the Charter on expropriation, and of Article 3 on the sharing of common resources, are closer to the influences at work in the contemporary world than the traditional rules that were applied in these awards.

Perhaps no firm conclusion can be drawn from these various considerations. But, even if it is accepted that Article 2 of the Charter reflects no change in the international law rules on the expropriation of foreign property, and if State practice is taken, as it must be, as the indicator, there is clear and widespread recognition that it would be politically imprudent to rely on customary rules of international law to secure the protection of foreign investments. Recourse must be had to specific agreements. By the middle of 1976 over one hundred such bilateral agreements had been concluded since 1962, between 12 industrialized countries and 34 less developed countries. The Federal Republic of Germany had agreements with 47 countries, of which 37 were in force by that time; Switzerland had 26 agreements in force, the US 12, the Netherlands 11, and France 8. Of the less developed countries Indonesia and Ivory Coast concluded the most agreements, 7 and 5 respectively.[106]

The agreements generally provide among other things for payment of adequate compensation in case of expropriation of any foreign investment and for the immediate and effective transfer of payment. For example, the *Belgium-Indonesia Agreement* (17.6.1972) provides for the following conditions to be met by any 'deprivation' of property, that:

(a) the measures are taken in the public interest and under due process of law in accordance with international law;
(b) the measures are neither discriminatory nor contrary to a specific engagement;
(c) the measures are accompanied by provisions for the payment of just compensation.

The amount of such compensation shall represent the actual value of the affected goods on the date on which the measure was taken. It shall be paid to the person entitled thereto and shall be freely transferable, without undue delay.

Sometimes no reference is made to international law, as here, though the agreement itself calls for conformity with domestic law. For example, the *Federal Republic of Germany–Zambia Agreement* (25.8.1972) says:

Art. 3. 1.   Investments by nationals or companies of either Contracting Party shall enjoy full protection as well as security in the territory of the other Contracting Party.
2.   Investments by nationals or companies of either Contracting Party shall not be expropriated in the territory of the other Contracting Party except for the public benefit and against compensation. Such compensation shall represent the equivalent of the investment expropriated; it shall be actually realizable, freely transferable, and shall be made without delay. Provision shall have been made in an appropriate manner at or prior to the time of expropriation for the determination and the giving of such compensation. The legality of any such expropriation and the amount of compensation shall be subject to review by due process of law.

A similar provision is to be found in the *United Kingdom–Egypt Agreement* (provisionally in force from 11.6.1975):

Art. 5. 1. Investments of nationals or companies of either Contracting Party shall not be nationalized, expropriated or subjected to measures having effect equivalent to nationalisation or expropriation (hereinafter referred to as 'expropriation') in the territory of the other Contracting Party except for a public purpose related to the internal needs of that Party and against prompt, adequate and effective compensation. Such compensation shall amount to the market value of the investment expropriated immediately before the expropriation itself or before there was an official Government announcement that expropriation would be effected in the future, whichever is the earlier, shall be made without delay, be effectively realizable and be freely transferable. The national or company affected shall have a right, under the law of the Contracting Party making the expropriation, to prompt review, by a judicial or other independant authority of that Party, of whether the expropriation is in conformity with domestic law and of the valuation of his or its investment in accordance with the principles set out in this paragraph.

Though the payment of compensation is more carefully regulated, the provisions of both these Agreements are otherwise similar to Article 2 of the Charter, in relying on domestic law and procedure for the protection of investments. The US has concluded relatively few agreements and their language is not always consistent: for example, the *Treaty of Friendship and Commerce with Pakistan* (12.2.1961) provides that:

Article 6 (4). Property of nationals and companies of either Party shall not be taken within the territories of the other Party except for a public purpose, nor shall it be taken without the prompt payment of just compensation. Such compensation shall be in an effectively realizable form and shall represent the full equivalent of the property taken; and adequate provision shall have been made at or prior to the time of taking for the determination and payment thereof.

But the *Treaty of Amity and Commercial Relations with Thailand* (8.6.1968) expressly invokes international law:

Article 3 (2). Property of nationals and companies of either Party, including direct or indirect interests in property, shall receive the most constant protection and security within the territories of the other Party. Such property shall not be taken without due process of law or without payment of just compensation in accordance with the principles of international law.

Further, the US Department of State declared its policy in December 1975:

Under international law the United States has a right to expect that any taking of American private property will be non-discriminatory
that it will be for a public purpose; and
that its citizens will receive prompt, adequate and effective compensation from the expropriating country.
... Acceptance by US nationals of less than fair market value does not constitute acceptance of any other standards by the US Government. As a consequence the US Government reserves its rights to maintain international claims for what it regards as adequate compensation under international law for the interests nationalised or transferred.

So much for the indications of State practice, showing widespread recourse to specific agreements. The principal enterprises have also been resorting to contractual means of protection of their investments and operations. The extractive industries have been perhaps the most vulnerable to expropriation and other nationalization measures in the less-developed countries. Many kinds of arrangement have been made, which have radically altered the relationships between the host State and the foreign enterprise. Contracts are concluded for joint ventures, equity sharing, and production or output sharing, or may take the form of service contracts.[107] It may be presumed that it is the internal law of the host State which governs such contracts.

The GATT

Economic power may of course be used, not only for influence and coercion, but simply to secure trade advantages. An ancient monopoly was the reservation of all colonial trade to English vessels by the Navigation Acts 1651–1660, and the Staple Act (1653) limiting colonial imports to English products. Trade preferences were even older, making one country the 'most-favoured' nation of another; and the colonial trade monoply of Britain was gradually transformed into the Commonwealth preference system. At the Imperial Economic Conference (1932) the UK undertook to maintain duty-free entry for Commonwealth goods; margins of preference of 10 per cent for imports from the Commonwealth of wheat flour, macaroni, barley, copra and asbestos; special preferences for imports from the Commonwealth of coffee, sugar, tobacco and wine; and to introduce new duties on imports of certain foreign agricultural products. The Commonwealth preference system was not unique. Similar preferences had been established between the territories of the French union, and on a basis of reciprocity—some discrimination was practised between Commonwealth countries—and also between the Belgium-Luxembourg customs union, the Netherlands, and the overseas territories of Belgium and the Netherlands; and between the US, its dependent territories, and the Philippines.

As the Second World War advanced it was seen that a great collective effort would be needed not only for the reconstruction of countries damaged by war, but for aid to many countries, in which economic development was only beginning; and there was also hope that there could be better management of international trade and payments than there had been between the two world wars, for there is virtually no country or territory that can be economically self-sufficient and not depend in some degree on international trade. Thirty years later the goal had not changed, and at an early stage of the Tokyo round it was declared that:

The goal is ... clear. It is to make economic interdependence, which is inescapable in the modern world, a more manageable and less troubling condition: or, what is the same thing, it is to find a range of livable compromises between the legitimate claim of national sovereignty and the imperatives of international order.

The Bretton Woods Conference had, a generation earlier, sought to create an international order, in which this goal could be reached. Using in part legal rules and structures, the Conference designed two related institutions: the International Bank for Reconstruction and Development (IBRD or World Bank) and the International Monetary Fund (IMF). J. M. Keynes, one of the architects of these institutions, when asked what the difference was between them, replied that you had to understand that the Bank was a fund, and that the Fund was a bank. In other words, IBRD resources were to be used to finance, by way of contracted loans to countries, post-war reconstruction and then projects, and later programmes, of economic development; while the IMF was to be an international central bank, in which the central banks or other monetary authorities in contributor member countries could obtain in effect overdrafts to meet balance of payments difficulties. The overdraft is constituted by the drawing of chosen foreign currencies in exchange for payment in national currency, that payment having to be redeemed in a given period. A third institution was to be the International Trade Organization, founded in the Havana Charter, which was the title given to the draft international agreement, worked out in Havana in 1948, on the trade rules and constitution of the ITO. But it was aborted by the refusal of the US Congress to approve US participation, a mark of the dominance of US economic power which was to endure for the next two decades.

Nevertheless, a large number of the provisions of the Havana Charter were incorporated after further negotiations in the General Agreement on Tariffs and Trade (GATT), which came provisionally into force between 23 countries, including the US and to which over eighty countries are now parties. The GATT is both in form and practice an illuminating example of law in international relations. It was virtually a harmonization of policies of the industrialized countries, which were the large part of the original participants and had the formative role in the construction of the Agreement. It was given the framework of a treaty, and the participating countries were duly described as contracting parties, but it cannot be read as a set of mutual rights and obligations. The conflicts of interests between national policies are such that the harmonization of policies can be best, and often only, achieved by consensus, not contract; and the GATT, not drafted with the elegance and precision of the Rome Treaty, is a subtle and effective expression of this. Hudec has well described it as '... designed and operated as a system of diplomacy.... adjudication, and to some extent even legislation, are not the terminal events one is accustomed to look for in more conventional systems. They are rather stages of a continuous process, in which there is usually more than one answer in the air at any one time.'[108] The GATT system is illustrated both in the range of its provisions aimed at good management of international trade and in the mode of resolution of conflicts that arise under the Agreement.

The provisions range from rules of administration, embodied in the domestic law of the contracting parties, through agreed standards to be observed in international trade, to recommended common policies. Among the rules are those covering freedom of transit;

imposition of fees and charges on imports and exports; marks of origin; the publication of trade regulations; and national treatment on international taxation and regulation. Certain standards of trade are obligatory; there is the generalization of most-favoured-nation treatment: Article I–1; the grant of negotiated and scheduled tariff concessions: Articles II, XXVIII; and the requirement that, since exchange control and trade regulation can have similar economic effects, the one shall not be used to evade or frustrate the standards governing the other: Article XV–4. The recommended common policies are elaborate and flexible, combining the expansion of multilateral trade with a fair protection of national interests, and depending on consensus rather than coercion, on consultation rather than adjudication.

The treatment in the GATT of quantitative restrictions is typical, occupying four lengthy Articles in seven pages of text. The general elimination of quantitative restrictions (QR) on imports or exports of products is made obligatory: Article XI–1. But, apart from the enumeration of a number of restrictions which are not to rank as QR, import restrictions may be introduced or intensified by a country 'to forestall the imminent threat of, or to stop, a serious decline in its monetary reserves . . . or . . . to achieve a reasonable rate of increase in its reserves': Article XII–1, 2. However, the use of QR, including these exceptionally allowed, must be non-discriminatory, aiming at 'a distribution of trade [in the product affected] approaching as closely as possible the shares which the various contracting parties might be expected to obtain in the absence of such restrictions', and criteria are set out that must be met by such restrictions: Article XIII. Yet again, there are specific exceptions to the rule of non-discrimination. To assess the consistency with the GATT of a particular set of QR, employed by a country, will be then a difficult task, calling for a good deal of economic analysis. As may be expected, consultation with the CONTRACTING PARTIES is called for at each stage. Where the term 'contracting parties' is spelt in capital letters in the GATT it refers to them as *acting jointly*, since the GATT was not given the same institutional structure as organizations like the IMF and IBRD. Consultation can be of two kinds: consultation required by the GATT itself, and consultation initiated by an individual country. So any participating country instituting or increasing the level of QR, to protect its balance of payments shall immediately consult the CONTRACTING PARTIES 'as to the nature of its balance of payments difficulties, alternative corrective measures which may be available, and the possible effect of the restrictions on the economies of other contracting parties'. The CONTRACTING PARTIES may indicate any inconsistency they find between the measures and provisions of the Agreement and 'may advise that the restrictions be suitably modified'. If however the inconsistency is considered serious and 'damage to the trade of any contracting party is threatened thereby', appropriate recommendations may be made for securing conformity with the Agreement provisions 'within a specified period of time'. If these are not complied with, a sanction can follow in that the CONTRACTING PARTIES may 'release any contracting party the trade of which is adversely affected by the restrictions, from such obligations under this Agreement towards the contracting party applying the restrictions', as they think appropriate. A similar process follows any complaint, initiated by any contracting party that establishes a *prima facie* case that certain QR are inconsistent with the Agreement and are adversely affecting its trade. Article XXIII also provides for hearing of complaints of nullification or impairment of trade interests by the action of a contracting party. Over 20 panel hearings have taken place, complete removal of the offending measures or a compromise being reached in a substantial number.

The pattern of settlement of disputes was in the first years of the GATT to set up working parties, composed of representatives of the countries in conflict and of a number of other countries, necessarily 'neutral'. Forty disputes were so handled between 1952 and 1958, the task of the working parties, ranging in size from 5 to 18 representatives, being to try to reach informed agreement. A single Panel on Complaints was then established, composed of six countries: Australia, Canada, Ceylon, Cuba, Finland and the Netherlands 'to consider, in consultation with the representatives of the countries directly concerned and of other interested countries, complaints referred . . . and to submit findings and recommendations to the CONTRACTING PARTIES'. Characteristic also is the GATT Arrangement regarding International Trade in Textiles. Under it there is a Textiles Committee, which makes an analysis of world trade and production in textile products, based on information provided by GATT contracting parties, and submits an annual review to the GATT Council. There is also established a Textiles Surveillance Body, which decides in cases stated on the conformity of the country's measures with the Arrangement. Composed of representatives of eight contracting parties, selected annually to give a fair balance to importing and exporting interests, it works by consensus, though the party to a dispute has no veto.

The GATT has been perhaps weakened over the last twenty years or so by, for example, the European Community treaties of *association*, a large extension of the concept of free-trade areas permitted in the GATT; the addition of a new Part IV to the Agreement releasing 'developing countries', inadequately defined, from a number of obligations as contracting parties; the adoption of the Generalized System of Preferences in 1971, which required and obtained a ten-year waiver of the obligation to grant general most-favoured-nation treatment; the use of embargo policies by the US and OAPEC; and the increase of protectionism[109] in the industrialized countries. Nevertheless, the GATT survives and remains a model of law as process—an amalgam of specific obligations, codes of conduct, and commercial policy recommendations, working through consensus and organized persuasion.

4 Human Rights

The collective responses to national behaviour, including UN action, lead us to another confrontation of law and power—the protection of human rights from the abusive exercise of national power, domestically or internationally.

Such collective responses are largely stimulated and governed by the increasing interdependence of countries, and the reduction of national barriers, political and cultural. But forms of response can still be open to challenge, as we shall see later, by reliance on the principle of non-intervention in the internal affairs of other countries. Further, since the use of force has as far as possible to be avoided, action will in the first stage take forms of influence or coercion, often economic.

The UN Charter has generalized the principle of collective security, by treating the maintenance of international peace and security as a common interest. A threat to the peace, or breach of the peace, wherever located and however constituted, is now the concern of all; and UN peacekeeping is a means of serving that common interest. But we shall not attempt any extended description of UN peacekeeping here.[110] In the UN system there have been parallel generalizations in the common interest of other principles of State conduct: of good neighbourliness, of the need for fair distribution and prudent management of natural resources, and of minimum standards of domestic behaviour. These principles are already recognized in regularities of behaviour and are also coming to be expressed in rules and standards, functioning as law. We shall now try to see what is the authority or influence of law in the international control of the exercise of State power, when it can be seen to be infringing such common interests or standards. International control may, as we shall see, take a number of forms of varying effectiveness and may often have to face the invocation of the principle of non-intervention in the internal affairs of States.

91

Rhodesia (1965–   )

A striking example of protection of human rights is the international handling of the situation in Southern Rhodesia from 1965.

Collective interventions for humanitarian reasons had taken place in the nineteenth century,[111] and the League Mandates system made limited provision for non-discrimination and political progress in the government of some dependent territories. But it would have doubtless surprised the drafters of the League Covenant, and even of the UN Charter, to be told that the first use of mandatory economic sanctions would be not to prevent or reduce an act of external aggression, but to change an internal regime of 'racist minority settlers'.

Rhodesia was formed in the last decade of the nineteenth century in a northward thrust of commerce and exploitation of mineral resources, in which Cecil Rhodes was a leader, his eyes straining, as it was said, from the Zambesi to the Nile. The British South Africa Company was granted a royal charter in 1889, giving it some of the status of the East India Company. The objects of the Company recognized under the charter were:

> To undertake and carry on the government or administration of any territories, districts or places, in Africa, and generally to exercise all rights and powers granted by or exercisable under the Charter, and particularly to improve, develop and cultivate, any lands included within the territories of the Company, and to settle any such territories and lands.

By 1893 the Company had, under the stimulus of Cecil Rhodes, acquired both Mashonaland and Matabeleland, and the combined territories were named after him in 1896. A constitution granted by Order-in-Council in 1898 provided for a legislative assembly, with a minority of elected members, and reserved to the British Government control over 'native affairs'. But Company administration continued over Rhodesia, divided in 1911 into Northern and Southern, until the royal charter expired in 1914.

The acquisition of the territory of Southern Rhodesia by the Company was later described by the Judicial Committee of the Privy Council as conquest, and an act of the Crown:

> Those who knew the facts at the time did not hesitate to speak, and rightly so, of conquest, and if there was a conquest by the

Company's arms, then by well-settled constitutional practice, that conquest was on behalf of the Crown.[112]

A public referendum held in Southern Rhodesia in 1922 rejected a proposal that it be incorporated in South Africa, and the territory became a self-governing colony in 1923. The Legislative Council had had an unofficial majority from 1920, though there was provision for reservation of Bills for assent of the Westminster Parliament, if they appeared to infringe African interests. The Governor was appointed on the advice of the Prime Minister of Southern Rhodesia, and all public servants were appointed by, and were solely responsible to, its Government. There appears to be little reason why Southern Rhodesia should not have been regarded as having the same independent status as Canada, the reservation of Bills being no different in range or effect from the requirement of UK legislation for the amendment of certain provisions of the Canadian constitution under the British North America Acts. It was repeated in the Constitution of the Federation of Rhodesia and Nyasaland established in 1953.

But political control from Westminster of a largely self-sufficient country, land-locked and lying away from the old imperial bases and lines of communication, was plainly never welcome or strongly asserted. In no case between 1923 and the dissolution of the Federation in 1963 did the reservation of Bills lead to action by the UK Government or Parliament for the protection of Africans in Southern Rhodesia. A Federal Constitutional Amendment Bill, and an Electoral Bill, were both referred by the African Affairs Board to the Westminster Parliament as being in the opinion of the Board 'differentiating' under Article 77 of the Constitution (1953), that is to say, discriminatory. But Parliament allowed both Bills, an Opposition (Labour) motion to disallow the first Bill being defeated by 301–245 votes.

A Joint Declaration of the UK Government and the Federal Government in April 1957 invokes a 'convention' which might appear on the face of it to be inconsistent with the Federal Constitution provisions for reservation of certain Bills:

The United Kingdom recognises the existence of a convention applicable to the present stage of the constitutional evolution of the Federation, whereby the United Kingdom in practice does not initiate any legislation to amend or repeal any Federal Act or to deal with any matter included within the competence of the

93

Federal legislature except at the request of the Federal Government.

Some of the language ('applicable to the present stage': 'in practice') suggests that the 'convention' is not a rule or principle of consitutional law, but simply describes a policy of expedience applicable or not according to the circumstances. Alternatively, a distinction might be being drawn between ordinary domestic legislation in a self-governing colony, and legislation modifying its constitutional status; the convention of non-interference by the Westminster Parliament would then be applicable to the first and not the second; and the Westminster Parliament would retain the political power to change the status of a colony. The constitutional practice appears to confirm this approach. The Constitution of Southern Rhodesia (1961) enabled the legislature to enact any statute whatsoever, provided it did not affect the position of the Sovereign or the Governor, and it also curtailed the power of disallowance.[113] An alteration of the relation between the Sovereign and Southern Rhodesia, for example, by declaration of a republic, could not then be achieved by Federal legislation; and in the words of the United Kingdom Government in 1964, 'a mere declaration of independence would have no constitutional effect. The only way Southern Rhodesia can become a sovereign independent State is by an Act of the British Parliament.' The British Caribbean Federation was dissolved by the West Indies Act 1962, not only not at the request of the Federal Government then in office, but against its declared will. Similarly, the Federation of Rhodesia and Nyasaland itself was dissolved on 31 December 1963, in face of strong opposition from the Federal Government. In this dissolution, described as 'an exercise of Britain's sovereign power',[114] policy was stronger than any constitutional convention. The practice shows then that the two interpretations suggested of the declaration are not in fact so very far apart. For the modification of the constitutional status of colonies—by dissolution of a federation or declaration of independence—is in practice an exercise of power, which is governed by political expedience and not by law, though it may be cast in legal forms.

So between 1963 and 1965 we see the first phase of confrontation of law and power in the relations between the United Kingdom and the self-governing colony of Southern Rhodesia. In law, the independence of Southern Rhodesia could be attained only through the total withdrawal of the legislative authority of the Westminster Parlia ment, following the pattern of independence legislation enacted for British colonies in the previous decade. But the power of the UK had been attenuated, by its long non-intervention or indifference over the internal affairs of Southern Rhodesia, constituting a recognition in practice of its virtual independence. Here another part of the Joint Declaration of April 1957 is relevant:

> The Federal Prime Minister represented that the time had come for the Federation to assume more responsibility . . . particularly in the field of relations with other countries and the appointment of representatives of the Federation in such countries. The United Kingdom Government have agreed to entrust responsibility for external affairs to the Federal Government to the fullest extent possible consistent with the responsibility which H.M. Government must continue to have in international law so long as the Federation is not a separate international entity.

The record shows on the one hand that the Federation and Southern Rhodesia conducted external relations at many points,[115] though they did not claim or receive any recognition as independent States; but, on the other hand, that this was to be attributed not to a lack of qualification of Southern Rhodesia to be an independent State but to constitutional limitations accepted by it. Upon the unilateral declaration of independence in 1965, the United Kingdom, lacking the power of effective intervention and refusing to recognize the legal discontinuity that had been created, had recourse to the legal fiction of the Southern Rhodesia Act (1965), purporting to re-establish the pre-1923 status of the territory.

The second phase of confrontation of law and power took place in the United Nations. The 'Committee of 24', established to implement General Assembly Resolution 1514–XV on decolonization, had been preoccupied with Rhodesia and the General Assembly itself adopted a number of Resolutions on it in 1962–3. The UK maintained both that Rhodesia was not a 'self-governing territory' in the sense of Article 73 and that Article 2(7) precluded UN intervention in its affairs as being within the domestic jurisdiction of the UK; further in the words of the UK delegate in the General Assembly which adopted Resolution 1755–XVII (12.10.1962),[116] the relationship between the United Kingdom and Rhodesia was 'something halfway between dependence and independence' and as 'not executive but primarily diplomatic in character'.[117]

The General Assembly rejected these suggestions and took its stand on Article 73 of the Charter,[118] insisting both that Rhodesia was in fact a non-self-governing territory and also that the UK was the administering power. As to the first the UN was asserting the political reality, to be recognized in effect by the UK itself in the *Tiger* proposals of December 1966.[119] These enunciated six principles as the basis of a recognizable independence for Rhodesia:

immediate improvement in the political status of the African population;

unimpeded progress to majority rule;

guarantees against retrogressive amendment of the Constitution (1961);

progress towards ending racial discrimination;

no oppression, regardless of race, of majority by minority or of minority by majority;

acceptance by the people of Rhodesia as a whole of any basis proposed for independence.

The relevance of these principles could not be contested. Although the Africans outnumbered the Europeans by sixteen to one in a population of over 4 million, less than 1 per cent of the registered voters in 1953 were African; and the Lands Apportionment Acts (1936, 1941) had allotted some 50,000 square miles to 2,630,000 Africans, and 75,000 square miles of mostly better land to 215,000 Europeans. Further, the Law and Order (Maintenance) Act was habitually used to restrict African political activity.

But in persisting in a series of Resolutions[120] in the attribution of administrative authority in Rhodesia to the UK, the General Assembly itself confused responsibility and power, and law with its enforceability. The UK had no power to carry out such constitutional responsibility as it might have for the conduct of internal affairs in Rhodesia, and no means to enforce any legislative measures it might adopt. The Security Council, brought into the act in May 1965 by the 'Committee of 24', appeared in part to recognize this for it adopted Resolution 202, requesting UN members to refuse recognition of any declaration of independence by the 'minority government', requesting the UK not to transfer to:

its colony of Southern Rhodesia as at present governed any of the power or attributes of sovereignty, but to promote the country's attainment of independence with a democratic system of government in accordance with the aspirations of the majority of the population and calling for a constitutional conference. The fact that 'all powers and attributes of sovereignty' were already possessed by Rhodesia, save in respect of the role of the Queen and Governor, wholly nominal in a Commonwealth of monarchies and republics, was ignored by the Security Council.

As negotiations between the UK and Rhodesian Governments showed no progress, and the threat of the latter to seize independence increased, the General Assembly passed two Resolutions on 12 October 1965 and 5 November 1965, the second going further than any earlier UN Resolutions; for it called upon the UK to 'employ all necessary means, including military force' to effect the release of all political detainees, the repeal of repressive or discriminatory legislation, including the Law and Order (Maintenance) Act and the Lands Apportionment Acts, and the 'removal of all restrictions on African political activity, and the establishment of full democratic freedom and equality of political rights'. How the UK was to do this was not made clear. On 11 November 1965 the Rhodesian Government made a unilateral declaration of independence of Rhodesia and became the illegal Smith régime. The legal discontinuity remained until 1979, when by a working arrangement between the UK Government and the Muzorewa Government, still illegal in British Constitutional law but not in Rhodesian law, British rule was restored on a temporary basis.[121]

After UDI the confrontation of law and power became centred around the conference of the UN to intervene in Rhodesia through the Security Council, by supporting and extending UK action against the illegal régime, and the effectiveness of mandatory economic coercion. On the day following UDI the UK not only abandoned its earlier plea that UN intervention was precluded by Article 2(7) of the Charter, but itself invited the Security Council to talks. In addressing the Council,[122] the British Foreign Secretary asked for support in discharging the 'British responsibility to re-establish the rule of law in Southern Rhodesia', for two main reasons:

The first reason is this. An attempt to establish in Africa an illegal régime based on minority rule is a matter of world concern. . . . The second reason why we now bring the matter before this Council is a severely practical reason. I am about to describe the measures which the United Kingdom Government has taken to deal with this illegal declaration and to restore the rule of law in

Southern Rhodesia. If these measures are to be fully effective we must ask for the good will, the cooperation and the active support of all those who accept the principle set out in Resolution 2012 (XX) adopted by the General Assembly on 12 October 1965 by a vote of 107 to 2.

The measures included prohibition of export of arms to Rhodesia, and of the import of tobacco and sugar from it to the UK; imposition of exchange restrictions and denial of Rhodesian access to the London capital market; and denial of trade advantages to Rhodesia under the Ottawa Agreement, Commonwealth preferences, or export credits. The Security Council response was cautious, and Resolution 216 (12.11.1965), adopted by 10–0 (France abstaining) said no more than that it:

1. Decides to condemn the unilateral declaration of independence made by a racist minority in Southern Rhodesia;
2. Decides to call upon all States not to recognize this illegal racist minority régime in Southern Rhodesia and to refrain from rendering any assistance to this illegal régime.

Wide dissatisfaction with this Resolution led to the submission of a far stronger draft Resolution by African delegations, and after several days of negotiation and amendment Resolution 217 (20.12.65) was adopted by the same vote as Resolution 216. It went beyond the earlier in a number of ways, where the Security Council:

1. Determines that the situation resulting from the proclamation of independence by the illegal authorities in Southern Rhodesia is extremely grave, that the Government of the United Kingdom of Great Britain and Northern Ireland should put an end to it and that its continuance in time constitutes a threat to international peace and security;
4. Calls upon the Government of the United Kingdom to quell this rebellion of the racist minority;
5. Further calls upon the Government of the United Kingdom to take all other appropriate measures which would prove effective in eliminating the authority of the usurpers and in bringing the minority régime in Southern Rhodesia to an immediate end;
8. Calls upon all States to refrain from any action which would assist and encourage the illegal régime and, in particular, to desist from providing it with arms, equipment and military

material, and to do their utmost in order to break all economic relations with Southern Rhodesia, including an embargo on oil and petroleum products;

9. Calls upon the Government of the United Kingdom to enforce urgently and with vigour all the measures it has announced, as well as those mentioned in paragraph 8 above;

This Resolution, despite the cautious observation that the 'continuance in time' of the Rhodesian situation was a threat to international peace under Article 39[123] of the Charter, was still composed of recommendations, no decision being made that UN members must implement under Article 25. But in addition to extending the list of prohibited imports from Rhodesia to the UK, and tightening the restrictions on money movements, the British Government, exercising powers conferred by the Southern Rhodesia Act (1965), proscribed the importation of oil to Rhodesia, and established a naval patrol in the Mozambique Channel to prevent it, particularly through the port of Beira. The first challenge was the arrival at Beira of the *Joanna V*, and the approach of the *Manuela* believed to be carrying 16,000 tons of oil for Rhodesia at the beginning of April 1966.

On 5 April *Joanna V*, a tanker flying the Greek flag, entered Beira fully laden with crude oil from the Persian Gulf, destined presumably for the Umtali pipeline. The master had refused a request by a British frigate not to enter Beira. The British Government then made representations to both the Portuguese and Greek Governments not to permit the vessel to unload its cargo at Beira. The Greek Government replied that it did not know who the owner of the vessel was, but cancelled its Greek registry on the ground that it was in breach of Royal Decree prohibiting carriage of oil to Rhodesia. The vessel was recommissioned in Panamanian registry, but did not unload, dropping another two miles offshore. Portugal, which had, with South Africa, voted against General Assembly Resolution 2012–XX, replied that land-locked states had a right of access to the sea and that oil arriving in Mozambique would be allowed to be moved to its destination. The British Government asked for an emergency meeting of the Security Council, which on 7 April 1966 adopted Resolution 221, directed against the supply of oil to Rhodesia. The Security Council voted in favour of the Resolution proposed by the UK by 10–0 with 5 abstentions,[124] saying:

Considering that such supplies will afford great assistance and encouragement to the illegal régime in Southern Rhodesia, thereby enabling it to remain longer in being.

1. Determines that the resulting situation constitutes a threat to the peace;
2. Calls upon the Portuguese Government not to permit oil to be pumped through the pipeline from Beira to Southern Rhodesia;
3. Calls upon the Portuguese Government not to receive at Beira oil destined for Southern Rhodesia;
4. Calls upon all States to ensure the diversion of any of their vessels reasonably believed to be carrying oil destined for Southern Rhodesia which may be en route for Beira;
5. Calls upon the Government of the United Kingdom of Great Britain and Northern Ireland to prevent, by the use of force if necessary, the arrival at Beira of vessels reasonably believed to be carrying oil destined for Southern Rhodesia, and empowers the United Kingdom to arrest and detain the tanker known as the Joanna V upon her departure from Beira in the event her oil cargo is discharged there.

Immediately after the adoption of the Resolution, a British frigate, HMS *Berwick*, intercepted the *Manuela* in the Mozambique Channel, put on a boarding party and accompanied her for some time on passage to Durban.

From May to December 1966 efforts to achieve a negotiated settlement, culminating in the *Tiger* proposals, were made by British and Rhodesian representatives. The principle of 'no independence before majority rule' (NIBMAR) became a central issue for interested Commonwealth countries; and at a meeting of Commonwealth Prime Ministers in September the UK undertook to support countermeasures, if no settlement with Rhodesia was reached in the negotiations. They broke down and the UK returned with a draft Resolution to the Security Council. On 16 December 1966 it adopted[125] under Chapter VII of the Charter Resolution 232, the first mandatory order for international sanctions. In its substantive provisions, the Security Council:

Acting in accordance with Articles 39 and 41 of the United Nations Charter,

1. Determines that the present situation in Southern Rhodesia constitutes a threat to international peace and security;
2. Decides that all States members of the United Nations shall prevent:

100

(a) The import into their territories of asbestos, iron ore, chrome, pig-iron, sugar, tobacco, copper, meat products and hides, skins and leather originating in Southern Rhodesia and exported therefrom after the date of this resolution;

(b) Any activities by their nationals or in their territories which promote or are calculated to promote the export of these commodities from Southern Rhodesia and any dealings by their nationals or in their territories in any of these commodities originating in Southern Rhodesia and exported therefrom after the date of this resolution, including in particular any transfer of funds to Southern Rhodesia for the purposes of such activities or dealings.

(c) Shipment in vessels or aircraft of their registration of any of these commodities originating in Southern Rhodesia and exported therefrom after the date of this resolution;

(d) Any activities by their nationals or in their territories which promote or are calculated to promote the sale or shipment to Southern Rhodesia of arms, ammunition of all types, military aircraft, military vehicles, and equipment and materials for the manufacture and maintenance of arms and ammunition in Southern Rhodesia.

(e) Any activities by their nationals or in their territories which promote or are calculated to promote the supply to Southern Rhodesia of the manufacture, assembly or maintenance of aircraft and motor vehicles in Southern Rhodesia: the shipment of vessels and aircraft of their registration of any such goods destined for Southern Rhodesia: and any activities by their nationals or in their territories which promote or are calculated to promote the manufacture or assembly of aircraft or of motor vehicles in Southern Rhodesia;

Notwithstanding any contracts entered into or licences granted before the date of this resolution;

(f) Participation in their territories or territories under their administration or in land or air transport facilities or by their nationals or vessels of their registration in the supply of oil or oil products to Southern Rhodesia.

3. Reminds Member States that the failure or refusal by any of them to implement this resolution shall constitute a violation of Article 25 of the Charter;

4. Reaffirms the inalienable rights of the people of Southern Rhodesia to freedom and independence in accordance with the declaration contained in General Assembly Resolution 1514 (XV); and recognizes the legitimacy of their struggle to secure the enjoyment of their rights as set forth in the Charter of the United Nations;

On 29 May 1968 the Security Council, '*Noting* with great concern that the measures taken so far have failed to bring the rebellion in Southern Rhodesia', and '*Gravely concerned* that . . . some States, contrary to Resolution 232 (1966) . . . have failed to prevent trade with the illegal régime in Southern Rhodesia', adopted Resolution 253 again under Chapter VII of the Charter. This Resolution repeated with some elaborations the substance of Resolution 232, but some paragraphs call for attention. The Security Council:

Acting under Chapter VII of the United Nations Charter,

1. *Condemns* all measures of political repression, including arrests, detentions, trials and executions which violate fundamental freedoms and rights of the people of Southern Rhodesia, and calls upon the Government of the United Kingdom to take all possible measures to put an end to such actions;

2. *Calls upon* the United Kingdom as the administering Power in the discharge of its responsibility to take urgently all effective measures to bring to an end the rebellion in Southern Rhodesia, and enable the people to secure the enjoyment of their rights as set forth in the Charter of the United Nations and in conformity with the objectives of General Assembly resolution 1514 (XV);

19. *Requests* the Secretary-General to report to the Security Council on the progress of the implementation of this resolution, the first report to be made not later than 1 September 1968;

20. *Decides* to establish, in accordance with rule 28 of the provisional rules of procedure of the Security Council, a committee of the Security Council to undertake the following tasks and to report to it with its observations;

    (a) To examine such reports on the implementation of the present resolution as are submitted by the Secretary-General;

    (b) To seek from any States Members of the United Nations or of the specialized agencies such further information regarding the trade of that State (including information regarding the commodities and products exempted from the prohibition contained in operative paragraph 3(d) above) or regarding any activities by any nationals of that State or in its territories that may constitute an evasion of the measures decided upon in this resolution as it may consider necessary for the proper discharge of its duty to report to the Security Council;

Nearly fifteen years were to pass before the Rhodesian régime was changed in the direction desired in the Security Council, so that mandatory sanctions, even though widely imposed, cannot be said to have materially influenced the change. Their effects, as has been suggested,[126] were probably rather to legitimize the guerrilla campaign and to discourage in some degree continuing white settlement in Rhodesia.

The protection of human rights also prompts some reflection on nuclear power. Nuclear power has several dimensions. It is a form of controllable energy; it is a source of economic power, when that energy can be effectively directed to industrial uses; and it is a form of politics—strategic power in nuclear weapons. A linkage of human rights and nuclear power is justified here because the efforts to bring nuclear power under the control of law have largely had their protection as the object, and because it shows that law can sometimes, at least in international relations, be invoked to reconcile incompatibles. The St. Petersburg Declaration (1868), an early step towards the establishment of laws of war, recognized the conflict between the dictates of humanity and military necessity, and the question which must prevail remains unanswered. President Truman was even able to plead the protection of human rights as justification of the dropping of the atomic bomb on Hiroshima. 'The first atomic bomb', he said, 'was dropped on Hiroshima, a military base, because we wished in this first attack to avoid, as far as possible, the killing of civilians.' The falsity of this is patent. Further, 'Having found the bomb, we have used it against those who attacked us without warning at Pearl Harbour, against those who have starved, beaten, and executed American prisoners, against those who have abandoned all pretence of obeying international laws of warfare.' So the indiscriminate killing of 70,000 people is, it appears, legitimate punishment of a community which has denied human rights to prisoners of war.

Finally, 'We have used it in order to shorten the agony of the war, in order to save the lives of young Americans.' Military necessity at last, seen again as the need to protect human lives.

The attitude to nuclear weapons has continued to be schizophrenic. The UN General Assembly has adopted two Resolutions, which would prohibit them as unlawful. So Resolution 1653–XVI (24.11.1961) declared that:

> ... any State using nuclear and thermonuclear weapons is to be considered as violating the Charter ..., as acting contrary to the laws of humanity, and as committing a crime against mankind and civilization ... the use ... would exceed even the scope of war and cause indiscriminate suffering to mankind and civilization.

Resolution 2936–XXVII (29.11.1972) also asserted 'the permanent prohibition of the use of nuclear weapons'. But the notion that these Resolutions are law-making, or even declaratory of the law, is quickly dispelled by the voting. The first was adopted by 55 votes, but 20 countries voted against and 26 abstained. The second won the support of 73 countries, but 4 were against, and no less than 46 countries showed uncertainty or indifference by abstaining. The Resolutions cannot be seen, then, as more than demonstrations of protest against nuclear weapons by a limited number of countries.

That nuclear weapons are not yet unlawful is evidenced further by the military manuals, for example, of the US and the UK, which state that the use of nuclear weapons against military objectives is not unlawful, and by the limited international conventions, which seek to bring them under some control. So the Antarctica Convention (1959), the Outer Space Treaty (1967) and the Sea-bed Treaty (1971) are confined to preventing the emplacement of nuclear weapons in certain regions of the Earth and of outer space, and the Treaty of Tlatelolco (1967) prohibits the use of nuclear weapons, or threat of their use, between the countries that are parties to it; 23 countries in Central and South America have ratified it, as well as China, France, the Netherlands, the UK and the US. The Non-Proliferation Treaty (1968) is designed to prevent the spread of nuclear weapons and of the means of their manufacture, but its system of safeguards, under which the International Atomic Energy Agency has concluded over 40 agreements, has many limitations as far as concerns the secrecy, inspection and accounting for materials, in nuclear weapons production. It may be that nuclear power in the form of weapons is becoming in fact a limitation on State power. As particular missiles become obsolete, being overtaken by technological advances, the more sophisticated missiles must then be designed, tested and produced, if the industrial complex is not to become stagnant; and so the production of increasingly sophisticated weapons becomes industrially an ascending spiral in which governments are imprisoned. Further, as Frank Barnaby has observed: 'The main function of those strategic weapons is . . . no longer the deterrence of war, but the deterrence of the use of strategic nuclear weapons.' In short, it is not possible to hold the arms race at given levels.

The review of the Rhodesian experience also shows some of the limits of power, and the tactical uses of law; and both will be briefly described. But it also compels further consideration of two related questions about the role of law in international relations: what is the scope of the principle of non-intervention in the internal affairs of a country; and can economic coercion be regarded in some circumstances as a use of force, possibly contrary to the UN Charter?

The limits of governmental power of Rhodesia and of the United Kingdom are visible in the failure to control insurgency and rebellion. The internal conflict was met by coercive measures, including detention and deportation; the Zimbabwe African Peoples Union (ZAPU) was banned in September 1962 and Joshua Nkomo, and other African leaders, imprisoned. But the gradual build-up of guerilla activities, based in neighbouring countries, was not prevented and after a decade of independence had become critical for the Rhodesian government. The instruments of coercion available to the UK after the declaration of independence, authoritatively described as 'treasonable and rebellious', were blunt or unusable: the exercise of constitutional and legislative authority, or military intervention. In fact, the limits of imperial power had long been recognized in colonial practice and in the legal forms of colonization: these ranged from annexation through protectorates and leased territory to capitulations and the grant of concessions, according to the degrees of possible control or geographical remoteness. The Chinese Empire was no exception. Its fringe territories were seen as territorially part of it, though in practice virtually autonomous. So in the Constitution (1975) the preamble states that 'Taiwan is China's sacred territory. We are determined to liberate Taiwan and accomplish the great cause of unifying our motherland'; and there is also significant reference to 'our compatriots in Hong Kong and Macao' in the consolidation and expansion of the 'revolutionary united front'.

The exercise of collective power through the UN had also its limits in Rhodesia variously imposed by the nature of the objective chosen, by the principle of non-intervention in internal affairs, and by the decline in the effectiveness of economic coercion. The real objective of the Security Council Resolutions, including the imposition of mandatory sanctions, was the overthrow of the 'illegal racist régime' in Rhodesia, or, in the idiom that has later become fashionable, the international protection of human rights. How was this objective to be brought within the UN Charter? How to reconcile the exercise of outside influence or coercion on States with the principle of non-intervention in their internal affairs has been long recognized as a difficult, if not insoluble, problem, once the use of force is to be abandoned.

The League Covenant recognized the reserved domain of States; for if an international dispute 'likely to lead to a rupture' is claimed by a party to it, and is found by the League Council, to which it has been submitted, 'to arise out of a matter which by international law is solely within the domestic jurisdiction of that party' the Council shall make no recommendations as to its settlement.[127] The UN Charter restated the principle in slightly broader language;[128] for what is 'solely within the domestic jurisdiction' of a State would, in at least a world of increasing interdependence, be a very limited field, while what is 'essentially within the domestic jurisdiction' can still include matters which are of international interest or concern, but which are nevertheless still to be kept out of reach of the UN. But there has been continuing disagreement over the scope of Article 2(7), and the extent of permissible intervention by the UN or individual States in internal affairs, and this will be further discussed below. However, different approaches to the issue of what intervention is permissible may converge on methods of intervention, although the purposes may differ or even be opposed. Intervention in a particular country may then be seen to be justified both on a liberal approach, where it is seen as the protection of human rights and on a socialist approach as a move against neo-imperialism. So Marx made a similar distinction, in terms perhaps more liberal than socialist, when he said in 1853 that: 'England has to fulfil a double mission in India: one destructive, the other regenerative—the annihilation of the old Asiatic society, and the laying of the foundations of Western society in Asia.'[129]

There was such a convergence of approaches over the situation in Rhodesia, leading to near consensus on the action to be taken. But given that the objective, however described, was to relieve the political and social condition of the African people, recourse had to be had to Chapter VII of the Charter, to avoid on the one hand the claim that these were matters within the domestic jurisdiction of the UK, and to devise measures on the other hand that could be effective. The claim having been in effect abandoned after the unilateral declaration of independence, the Security Council had recourse to Article 39, finding in Resolution 221 on the supply of oil to the illegal régime that 'the resulting situation constitutes a threat to the peace.' To speak of the *resulting* situation was still to project the situation into the future, to withhold a determination of the present, which was to be made in Resolution 232. That there should have been hesitation in describing the situation in Rhodesia after the declaration of independence as a threat to the peace was understandable. The Smith régime gave no sign of the use of force outside Rhodesia, and the anger of some African countries with the UK was directed precisely against its renunciation of the use of force, which they were unwilling or unable to embark upon themselves. But the exercise by the Security Council of a political and strategic judgement of what is a *threat* to the peace may be part of its peace-keeping, as distinct from its enforcement functions; it may be directed not to the actual use of force across a frontier, but to the prevention or control of actions likely to provoke a later use of force, regardless of who initiates them. In Rhodesia there was ground for a finding of a threat to the peace if only in the Rhodesian threat to compel immigrant workers from Malawi and Zambia to return home, and the infiltration into Rhodesia of armed irregulars from neighbouring territories.

But did not such peace-keeping itself require the use of force? Resolution 221 § 5 purported to authorize the use of force by the UK against foreign vessels on the high seas or in a foreign territorial sea. The deployment of HMS *Berwick* and its armed boarding party, which compelled the *Manuela* to alter course away from Beira, was certainly a use of force against a foreign vessel on the high seas; and it raises a number of legal questions. It might be said that, since its Greek registration had been officially cancelled in Greece, the *Manuela* was a stateless vessel not entitled to claim freedom of navigation on the high seas under the High Seas Convention (1962) Article 2(1) and (4). But Article 22(1) expressly fixes the conditions for arrest of a foreign merchant ship on the high seas, and the arrest of the *Manuela* did not satisfy any of those conditions; further, the vessel was not at that time acting or being used unlawfully, as was the *Asya*. Could then the Security Council, by what was in Resolution 221 a *recommendation* under Article 39, authorize action that would have been otherwise unlawful? It could be said that a recommendation for the use of force, strictly limited in purpose, scale, time and place, is a proper exercise by the Security Council of its responsibility under Article 24(1) of the Charter, and that it is then a collective act of UN members which none can challenge. It is of interest here that the Judicial Committee of the Privy Council observed in the case cited that, even if customary international law were invoked against the seizure of the *Asya*, 'it is far from clear that it would be applicable to the case of a Mandatory Power [the United Kingdom in Palestine] carrying out a common policy, the execution of which had been entrusted to it by other Powers.'

But the greatest limitation on the exercise of collective power is the decline in the effectiveness of international economic coercion. Before 1914 gunboats or a naval blockade or bombardment or invasion leading to war were the only instruments of power in the last resort:[130] in short, the use of force. A prime purpose of both the League Covenant and the UN Charter was to eliminate such uses of force between countries, and to prevent or penalize aggression and other international misconduct by economic sanctions. But the changes in the economic climate, at least since 1945, have been so great that such economic sanctions have become as difficult to design as they are to enforce. Susan Strange, in an unpublished study, identified these changes and their consequences.

First, there has been a steadily increasing interdependence not only between the internal sectors of advanced economies, but between the national sectors of economies at all levels. This is shown in the growth of transnational production processes and the large number of countries involved in the international market economy. Secondly, while there is a far greater involvement of government in most national economies, which might appear to make the imposition and enforcement of economic sanctions easier, this involvement focuses within government the conflict of national economic interests with a collective sanctions policy, so that government may support the policy in principle but withhold the restraints that could make it effective. Governments may issue regulations, designed to implement a collective sanctions policy by controlling the trade of enterprises within their jurisdiction. But what is the real range of that jurisdiction? While the multinational corporations may show themselves willing to cooperate in important trading areas, their complex structures, vertical and horizontal, can render such regulations meaningless. So the 'privateers', for example in shipping, can as Susan Strange stresses, be still the main operators against sanctions, since they are beyond control, save by limited blockade.

Thirdly, the capacity for economic self-defence against such imperfect economic coercion may be considerable. Loss of imports may be more easily borne than loss of exports and much can depend on the proportion of the two; further, if the impact of economic coercion is not speedily effective, time may allow substitutions and transfers of resources within the economy. These factors were stressed by the Committee of Exports, appointed by the Security Council in Resolution 191 (1964) to consider the feasibility of economic sanctions against South Africa. Observing that the substitution and redeployment of resources, as well as rationing, could be means of economic self-defence it said that:

it is not possible to draw precise conclusions as to the degree to which these measures or a combination of them might affect South Africa's economic activity, or as to the length of time it would take for their effects to be felt. The susceptibility of the South African economy to measures would vary from case to case, effectiveness being dependent upon the availability of measures of alleviation on the part of South Africa on the one side and an organised co-operative effort, including present and potential suppliers, on the other.[131]

In Rhodesia there was in fact expansion of the manufacturing industries after 1965, the volume of production being nearly doubled in the next decade; and both the Federal Republic of Germany and Switzerland, as non-members of the UN at the time, no doubt indirectly helped. It is recorded that between 1965 and 1974 Switzerland increased her imports from Rhodesia in value from $5678 million to $7352 million and exports to Rhodesia from $1641 million to $4546 million.[132]

The tactical use of law is exemplified both in the abandonment of legal positions when no longer politically material, and the avoidance of any conclusive determination of legal issues. So in the first phase of UN concern with the situation in Rhodesia, the UK invoked Article 2(7) of the Charter claiming that this excluded UN action since Rhodesia was within the domestic jurisdiction of the UK. Not only was this claim abandoned after UDI, but the UK took a directly contrary line in seeking UN support for its first measures of oil embargo against Rhodesia.

Further, a number of central questions were left unresolved in the UN process, none being referred to the International Court of Justice for an advisory opinion: for example, did normal principles of recognition of governments no longer apply to the Smith régime after UDI, since UN Resolutions created a new kind of non-recognition? Was the intervention of neighbouring States in Rhodesia justifiable? Can the Security Council legitimize the use of force by a recommendation, as distinct from a decision under Chapter VII? It was for political convenience taken for granted that the answer to these questions was positive.

5 Non-Intervention

Turning now to the scope of the principle of non-intervention in internal affairs, which has been already touched on in the discussion of the balance of power (p. 29), the reference to General Assembly Resolution 2625–XXV on the use of force (p. 46), and the UN action on Rhodesia (p. 92ff.), we must see how it has evolved and come to be understood, since the UN was established.

At least three kinds of intervention must be distinguished: intervention by the UN, collective intervention under a multilateral convention, and intervention by one or more States acting individually, though sometimes in consort. Collective intervention has already been described in one instance, where the OAS Convention was used and relied on to justify US naval action in the Cuban missiles crisis; and, since we are in this study looking more particularly at intervention by methods of economic coercion, it is the first and third kinds of intervention that will be compared. But it must also be kept in mind that the legitimacy of intervention must depend not only on its purpose but also on the methods used, both being obviously closely related.

Starting then with Article 2(7) of the UN Charter we see that of the other authentic texts, at least the French suggests a difference in referring to *affaires qui relévent essentiellement de la compétence nationale d'un Etat*. For matters within *la compétence nationale* could be understood as wider in extent than those within the 'domestic jurisdiction'. This would turn on distinguishing competence, as the power and authority to act, from jurisdiction, as the permitted area of action, though strictly speaking *compétence* in French may, like 'jurisdiction' in English, be used to express either idea. But whatever the merit of this distinction as a means of construction of the language used, it reflects a real difference on the interpretations of Article 2(7) in the UN. Following the distinction, it might be said that in Article 2(7) while 'domestic jurisdiction' would be naturally extended to cover the activities or movements abroad of nationals, including registered companies, and of flag vessels and aircraft, it could hardly comprise intervention by national armed forces in foreign territory. But such intervention might still be seen as coming within *la compétence nationale* under international law. For example, the intervention at Stanleyville in the Congo—now Kisangani in Zaire—by a unit of Belgian paratroops, carried in US military aircraft, was defended by the US in the Security Council on three grounds:[132] that it was authorized by the Congo Government; that it was conducted in conformity with the Geneva Conventions; and that it was an exercise of a clearly established responsibility to protect US citizens in the conditions obtaining at the time in the Stanleyville region. Much turns then on the qualification 'essentially' which takes the place of 'solely' in the parallel clause in the League Covenant.

In 1963 the General Assembly set up a Special Committee on the Principles of International Law concerning Friendly Relations and Cooperation between States to consider and make recommendations on four principles including 'the duty not to intervene in matters within the domestic jurisdiction of any State, in accordance with the Charter'. After much debate and controversy the issues passed to the First Committee and the General Assembly adopted Resolution 2131–XX (12.12.1965) on its recommendation, entitled Declaration on the Inadmissibility of Intervention in the Domestic Affairs of States and the Protection of their Independence and Sovereignty. The principle of non-intervention was stated in the following provisions, which were repeated, without essential change, in Resolution 2625–XXV (24.10.1970), and also in the Helsinki Final Act (1975) Principle VI.[133]

1. No State has the right to intervene, directly or indirectly, for any reason whatever, in the internal or external affairs of any other State. Consequently, armed intervention and all other forms of interference or attempted threats against the personality of the State or against its political, economic and cultural elements, are condemned.

2. No State may use or encourage the use of economic, political or any other type of measures to coerce another State in order to obtain from it the subordination of the exercise of its sovereign rights or to secure from it advantages of any kind. Also, no State shall organize, assist, foment, finance, incite or

tolerate subversive, terrorist or armed activities directed towards the violent overthrow of the régime of another State, or
interfere in civil strife in another State.

3. The use of force to deprive peoples of their national identity
constitutes a violation of their inalienable rights and of the
principle of non-intervention.

The UN debates on these Declarations, and international practice in
the last two decades reflect very different approaches to the principle
of non-intervention, which come from differing political attitudes.
They have already been described respectively as liberal and socialist,
the first expressing the ideas of liberal democracy, with which the
so-called West is sometimes identified, and the second those of
planned, sometimes authoritarian, societies.

On the liberal approach, it is said that the restriction of intervention in Article 2(7) applies only to the UN organs and not to particular States, acting individually or together; and that both Article
2(4)[134] and the UN Resolutions, as their terms indicate, are directed
primarily against the use of force, including the active support of
rebels aiming at the overthrow of an undesirable régime. Certain
forms of intervention are then permissible, provided the methods
fall short of the use of armed force, and the purpose is, for example,
the protection of human rights; and such intervention is within
national competence. It is here assumed that the declaration in the
Preamble of the UN Charter of intent 'to ensure, by the acceptance
of principles and the institution of methods, that armed force shall
not be used, save in the common interest', is directed to collective
action by the UN, in particular under Chapter VII of the Charter,
and to 'collective self-defence' against armed attack under Article 51.
It does not then imply that there can be other exceptions to the
prohibition of force in Article 2(4).

In the approach of many socialist countries, often shared by non-
aligned countries, it is said that the specific references to the use of
force do not themselves render other kinds of intervention permissible. On the contrary, the first sentence of paragraph 1 of
Resolution 2131–XX, repeated in Resolution 2625–XXV, is wholly
unqualified in its prohibition of intervention, direct or indirect, in
the internal or external affairs of any State; and the *condemnation* of
the use of force is a consequence not a characterization of the intervention that is forbidden. It is said further that Article 2(4) and (7)
together rest on the axioms of the political independence for States

E   113

and their exclusive jurisdiction over their affairs, and this being perhaps the key to the approach, that political independence for the majority of countries in the contemporary world, is freedom from neo-colonialism or, in the words of Brezhnev, from 'strategic plans against the world of socialism and the popular-liberation forces'.[135] These affairs are outside the jurisdiction of a State seeking to intervene.

But is the observance of certain minimum standards of government with respect to human rights and freedoms any longer essentially, still less exclusively, within the domestic jurisdiction of States? In situations where these are being reportedly ignored it has been the practice of the UN since its beginning to intervene, by public debate and the adoption of condemnatory Resolutions, or by full investigation where that is practicable, enforcement measures under Chapter VII being expressly permitted under Article 2(7). In effect this practice of intervention reflects the recognition by countries that they have a common interest in the protection of human rights; and further to serve such a common interest is a natural function of the UN.[136] But can States, acting individually, intervene in this common interest, given the prohibitions on intervention in the various Declarations just described? The answer will depend in part on how political independence is conceived. Brezhnev suggested in 1968 that intervention could sometimes be justified as serving a common interest: 'When internal and external forces that are hostile to socialism seek to reverse the development of any socialist country in the direction of restoring the capital system . . . that is no longer a problem for the people of that country, but also a common problem, a matter of concern for all socialist countries.'[137] But for China intervention by the US or USSR can itself be challenged: 'The people must see to it that these two superpowers . . . do not use force or the threat of force or other manoeuvres to interfere in their country's or any other country's internal affairs; moreover both powers must be clearly watched lest they resort to schemes of subversion, and use "aid" as a pretext to push through their military, political and economic plots.'[138]

Looking over this record of declarations and practice, we find no legal determination of the limits of intervention in terms of purpose. The UN Charter itself has nothing express to say about the principle of non-intervention; and if it is held that the General Assembly Resolutions have no force even as declarations of the law, the purposes of intervention remain uncontrolled. But as methods of intervention, the threat and use of force are excluded by the UN Charter if, for example, a portion of territory is to be taken over, or the government of the country is rendered incapable of making free political choices; and this principle is restated in the General Assembly Resolutions. Can then economic coercion rank as a use of force, or be otherwise prohibited? It must be noted, that the use of 'force' is mentioned four times in the UN Charter; and that in the Preamble, referred to above, and in Articles 41 and 46 covering action by the UN itself, the expression 'armed force/*la force armée*' is used, but in Article 2(4) it is simply 'force'. Further, the UN Resolutions 2131–XX and 2625–XXV, which must reflect at least a common understanding of Charter provisions, link economic coercion with 'armed intervention and all other forms of interference against the personality of the State or against its ... economic ... elements'; and declare that:

> No State may use or encourage the use of economic, political or any other type of measures to coerce another State in order to obtain from it the subordination of the exercise of its sovereign rights.

It is possible then that Article 2(4) could be extended to prohibit economic coercion which infringes or threatens the political independence of a State. But this is speculation and only broader conclusions can be drawn from this review of the principle of non-intervention.

It is evident that the increased political and economic interdependence of countries has reduced and is reducing the area of what can be said to be essentially within their domestic jurisdiction: for example, what are recognized as minimum standards of government with respect to human rights and freedoms have become universal. Nevertheless there can in practice be a conflict, indeed a contradiction, between the principle of self-determination—the free and sovereign choice by a country of its political and economic system—and the required observance of those minimum standards. This conflict may be removed or resolved in two ways. It may be held that the principle of 'self-determination of peoples', as declared for example in General Assembly Resolution 1514–XV (14.12.1960) and repeated verbatim in the first Article of each of the UN Covenants,[139] is directed essentially at the release of countries from colonialism and foreign rule, and that consequently the principle is no longer applicable to a country that has attained independence or entered into a free association with another country. This view is certainly held by many of the newly independent countries themselves, such as India, and had the approval of Secretary General U Thant. But it would then follow that an independent country cannot invoke the declared principle to escape international responsibilities in the choice of its political and economic system. A similar conclusion might be drawn from the UN Civil and Political Rights Covenant, which makes clear that the claim or exercise of rights involves responsibilities, stating that:

> Nothing in the present Covenant may be interpreted as implying for any State, group or person any right to engage in any activity or perform any act aimed at the destruction of any of the rights and freedoms recognized herein, or at their limitation to a greater extent than is provided for in the present Covenant.

The right of self-determination cannot then be invoked or used by countries, that have accepted the Covenant, to defend a régime which impermissibly restricts the rights and freedom of their inhabitants.

But the full extent of the principle of non-intervention in the internal affairs of other countries remains undetermined. The UN Charter prohibits the threat or use of force, as described above, and also permits intervention in certain circumstances by the UN itself. But there are no accepted rules of law either permitting or denying the use of economic coercion by States, acting individually, even to serve common interests, including the protection of human rights. Counter-measures may not then be excluded. So the US Export Administration (Amendment) Act (1977) prohibits any US national from complying with 'a boycott fostered or imposed by a foreign country against a country which is friendly to the US'.

6 An Opinion

Looking back over this brief review of the role of law in international relations, we find no unique set of propositions that can be called the law. Law is shaped, seen and used differently according to the context and the operators—parliamentarians, ministers and diplomats with their legal advisers, and judges.

The parliamentarian, coming to foreign affairs as debater or even as legislator, may not be much concerned with law, any more than his constituents. As Richard Nixon has observed: 'The average voter is not interested in the technicalities of treaty obligations. He thinks quite properly that Castro is a menace, and he favours the candidate, who wants to do something about it—something positive and dramatic and forceful—and not the one who takes the "statesmanlike" or "legalistic" view.'[140] But the ministers or diplomats and their legal advisers, closer to the forces at work, particularly in crisis, may have to be more statesmanlike or 'legalistic'. To recall our rough matrix, they are concerned to exercise influence or coercion in the national interest or common interest. These may be policy determinants. So the challenge to hegemony is expressed in a recent treaty between China and Japan, especially in Asia and the Pacific, and is favoured by an increasing number of countries; again there is the 'doctrine' of vital interests, as declared by Presidents Monroe, Eisenhower and Carter, and it is the nature of doctrine that it must be followed.

To be 'legalistic' is to make at least a tactical use of law. Legal claims and arguments can have diplomatic leverage, especially where treaty obligations can be invoked and their disregard may encounter reprisals. Further, crisis or conflict may be sometimes resolved by shifting it from the political to the legal plane: this can reduce the area of confrontation, make it easier for one side or the other to give way, and create an image of respect for the law. This last is politically important. National leaders, even dictators, like not only to give an appearance of being law-abiding, but to be able, when it is convenient, to charge an opponent country with breaches of international law; this can have a political impact on the public, even though it may generally regard international law as unreal and unenforceable. The other effects may also be kept in mind by international bodies. It has been well observed that the authority of international directives or recommendations, aiming at the resolution of conflict, will be the greater if certain conditions are met: that they cover a short period of time, seek to avoid further conflict or harm rather than find fault and call for measures of reparation, and call for some *acte juridique* but leave open other ways of pursuing legitimate interests.[141]

The international judge or arbitrator has a narrower function, to identify and apply the law, or decide *ex aequo et bono*. But in the identification of the law there can be an element of judicial legislation, and in its application to actual international disputes, if it is frequent and successful, international order may be fortified. What is sometimes called the Hague Court began as the Permanent Court of International Justice, wholly distinct from the Permanent Court of Arbitration, and was transformed into the present International Court of Justice in 1945, without substantial changes in its Statute. But the International Court of Justice has been used relatively less than its predecessor, particularly for advisory opinions. The reasons for this are disputed and certainly complex, but there are two factors about which there would probably be wide agreement. First, the exercise of the jurisdiction of the Court rests fundamentally and always on the consent of States. Acceptance of the compulsory jurisdiction of the Court has relatively declined. In 1939 over thirty countries had accepted it, or nearly three-quarters of the independent states then existing. But there has been no significant increase in the number of acceptances, and only a handful of the many countries that have become members of the UN since 1945 have made declarations of acceptance. Another aspect of the necessity for voluntary submission to the jurisdiction of the Court is that a number of preliminary objections to the exercise of that jurisdiction are open to the respondent State, and these are too often successful, given that acceptances of the jurisdiction are often made subject to reservations. Second, the institutionalization of international relations has opened the way to the handling of many disputes, by means both formal and informal, in international organizations themselves, and so still further reduced recourse to arbitral or judicial settlement; and here it is significant that UN Specialized Agencies have sought advisory opinions from the International Court in only two cases in thirty-five years.

The authority of law in international relations depends then rather less on its formation as rules than its function as part of the continuing processes of cooperation, exchange and conflict. Here, as we have seen, what functions as law embraces rules and obligations, recognized in long practice or specific agreements, and codes of conduct or harmonization of policies serving common interests. There are particular common interests both in predictability of behaviour in international relations and in the observance of at least minimum standards; no national interest can be secured without them. Such predictability is a factor both in the relations of any two countries and of the international community as a whole. George Kennan, speaking of the first in the context of US–USSR relations, has said that they rest 'on certain reassuring concepts of the motives and purposes of the other party, which it has taken long to establish but could be quickly shattered by confusing signals or abrupt changes in personality or behaviour at either end.'[142]

But the processes of international relations do not have a constant pattern. They are continuously and sometimes rapidly changing. The distribution of economic and politico-strategic power around the world has changed greatly even in the last two decades. Further, the confrontation with dramatic technological developments makes increasing demands on international law. The operation and uses of Earth satellites by their nature need global regulation, and the exploitation of the seabed, the need for better management of our natural environment and resources and, not least, nuclear power, require international action on a scale inconceivable in 1920. International law has been able to provide some usable concepts, which are still being developed, such as that of the common domain, the international regime, and the international corporate agency.

In sum, law cannot itself create order in international relations, but emerges as a fact of life where there are minimum degrees of order, which it may serve to rationalize and extend.

Notes

Abbreviations

AJIL   *American Journal of International Law*
BYIL   *British Yearbook of International Law*
ICJ   *International Court of Justice*

1 H. Bülck, 'Origins of Public International Law', in *Law and State* (Institute of Scientific Cooperation, Tübingen, 1977).
2 In recognition of custom as 'natural law', Themis ranked as a goddess older than Zeus.
3 See D. E. Roberts, *Existentialism and Religious Belief* (OUP, New York, 1959), Ch. V.
4 Nikos Kazantzakis is not far off when he says: 'That man is free who strives on earth with not one hope', quoted by John S. Dunne, *Time and Myth* (SCM Press, 1973), 35.
5 *The Federalist* (1788), X. For a contemporary study see Peter Singer, *Democracy and Disobedience* (OUP, 1973).
6 *Capital*, I, Ch. 24 (Primary Accumulation).
7 See M. C. Bassiouni, 'Prolegomenon to Terror Violence', in *Creighton Law Review* (Spring 1979), 745.
8 *Economic, Social and Cultural Rights Covenant* and *Civil and Political Rights Covenant*, which entered into force on 3.1.1976 and 23.3.1976 respectively. Fifty-four countries had ratified both Covenants by the end of 1978.
9 Ruth First, 'Uganda: the latest coup in Africa', *World Today* (March 1971), 136.
10 In a report in 1965 on the administration of the East African protectorates as they then were, it was observed that it was difficult in Kenya to persuade the people 'as a whole to recognise any one individual member of their tribe as a person of authority over them'. Quoted by D. A. Low, 'Lion Rampant', *Journal of Commonwealth Political Studies* (1965), 235.
11 Compare the observation of Kelsen that 'the State' is 'a name for the personification of a complex of rules'.
12 The terms were united by the Arbitrator in the *Island of Palmas Arbitral Award* [1928], 2 RIAA 839, when he said: 'Independence in regard to a portion of the globe is the right to exercise therein, to the exclusion of any other State, the function of a State. . . .'
13 *Rex* v. *Bottrill, ex pte Kuchenmeister* [1946], 1 AER 635; [1947], 1 KB 41 C.A.
14 UN Resolutions adopted in 1965 and 1966, after UDI, addressed the United Kingdom as the 'administering authority' of Southern Rhodesia.
15 [1969] 1 AC 644 PC.

16 *Ndhlovu* v. *The Queen* [1968], 2 South African Law Reports 535.

17 R. W. Cox and H. K. Jacobson, *The Anatomy of Influence* (1973), Appendices A and C.

18 *Decision-making in the White House* (Columbia UP, 1963).

18a *7 British International Law Digest*, 265.

19 *General Treaty for the Renunciation of War as an Instrument of National Policy*, signed in Paris on 27.8.1928; entered into force on 25.7.1929.

20 An unusual description after 1922.

21 *UN Charter*, Article 2(7).

22 *Cmnd 6964*, p. 30.

23 See the *Advisory opinion of the International Court of Justice on Reservations to the Genocide Convention* [1951], ICJ Reports 15; and the *Vienna Convention on the Law of Treaties*, Article 19(1).

24 Compare *Vienna Convention on the Law of Treaties*, Article 27.

25 *Cmnd 6198*, pp. 6, 52. Article 102 of the UN Charter requires the registration of 'every treaty and international agreement'.

26 This quotation, and that of Lord Palmerston, are taken from Martin Wight, *The Balance of Power and International Order* in *The Bases of International Order*, ed. Alan James (OUP, 1973), 27. See also B. Wassermann, 'The Balance of Power', *International Relations* (May 1977), 71.

27 See Alastair Buchan, *The End of the Postwar Era* (Weidenfeld and Nicolson, 1974), and particularly Ch. 4.

28 *North Atlantic Treaty*, Article 5, and *Warsaw Pact*, Article 14, are virtually identical here.

29 See Edward McWhinney, 'Peaceful coexistence and Soviet-Western international law', 56 *AJIL* (1962), 951.

30 The *Pacific Islanders Protection Act* [1875], ss. 6, 7 was to the same effect.

31 *Cmd 1617*.

32 *Nationality Decrees in Tunis and Morocco* [1923], PCIJ: B4 at 27. The English term 'protectorate' is in the context inexact.

33 *Rights of the United States Nationals in Morocco* [1952], ICJ Rep. 185.

34 Uganda was at one time composed of a protected State, Buganda, situated within a protectorate embracing three other communities.

35 The concept was developed by H. Duncan Hall, 'The International Frontier', 48 *AJIL* (1948), 142 and 'Zones of the International Frontier', 38 *Geographical Review* (1948), 615.

36 H. J. Morgenthau, *In Defense of the National Interest: A critical examination of American foreign policy* (Knopf, New York, 1951), 101.

36a *The Conventions of Crisis: A Study of Diplomatic Management* (OUP, 1971).

37 *Power Politics* (3rd edition, Stevens, 1964), 199.

38 For an illuminating account of Marxist thinking on international relations see F. Parkinson, *The Philosophy of International Relations* (Sage Publications, 1978), Ch. 7.

39 *de Jure Belli ac Pacis: Prolegomena*, § 22.

40 See Ivo Lapenna, 'Soviet concept of Socialist international law', 29 *Yearbook of World Affairs* (1975), 242.

41 Compare the observation of H. Lauterpacht that 'the will of the parties can never be the ultimate source of the binding force of a contract.' *Private Law Sources and Analogies of International Law* (OUP, 1927), 56.

42 'The Sanctions of International Law', 2 *AJIL* (1908), 451.

43 Trygve Lie in his sixth Annual Report to the General Assembly (1951) said: '. . . the peace and well-being of all nations and peoples have become in the present age so intimately interwelded that it is necessary for them, despite all their differences, to join in a world-wide organization looking towards

security from war, freedom and independence for the peoples, and mutual economic and social progress.'

44 See ICJ Advisory opinion on *Reparation for Injuries suffered in UN Services* [1949], ICJ Rep. 179. In *Nissau* v. *Attorney-General* [1967], 3 WLR 1044, Lord Denning MR described the UN as a 'Sovereign body corporate'.

45 We are not here considering resolutions having internal or constitutional effect within the UN, such as the adoption of Rules of Procedure under Article 21, the constitution of subsidiary organs under Article 22, or staff regulations. Such resolutions must be taken to have statutory force within the UN.

46 See G. Arangio-Ruiz, 'The Normative Role of the General Assembly of the UN and the Declaration of Principles of Friendly Relations', *Recueil des Cours* (III–1972).

47 Based in part on an earlier 'recommendation' (Resolution 637–VII: 16.12.1952) and elaborated in Resolution 1541–XV: 15.12.1960.

48 The texts were adopted by 107–0–2 (Portugal, South Africa). The Covenants both entered into force in 1976.

49 See p. 82.

50 See J. Gold, 'The "Sanctions" of the International Monetary Fund', 66 *AJIL* (1972), 737.

51 Article 94(1) of the Charter provides that: 'Each Member of the United Nations undertakes to comply with the decision of the International Court of Justice in any case to which it is a party.'

52 *Power and the Pursuit of Peace* (CUP, 1963), Ch. 4.

53 *Le Droit des Gens* (1758), III, Ch. iii § 47.

54 e.g. *Declaration of the UN Conference on the Human Environment* (June 1972)—Stockholm Declaration.

55 GA Resolution 2625–XXV, adopted on the twenty-fifth anniversary of the entry into force of the UN Charter.

56 The term 'irregular fighter', preferable to loaded terms such as 'terrorist' 'freedom fighter', is used by G. I. A. D. Draper, 'Status of Combatants and Guerrilla Warfare', 45 *BYIL* (1971), 183.

57 Romanes Lecture (1907). Quoted by Dorothy Woodman *Himalayan Frontiers* (Cresset Press, 1969), 6.

58 Li Fan Yüan (Frontier Control Bureau): George Moseley, *China's Search*, 303; 'The administrative autonomy enjoyed by the frontier dependencies of the Ch'ing empire was not inconsistent with the idea that they were in-trinsically part of China.'

59 A tributary entering the Amur a short distance east of the junction of the Shilka, Argun and Amur Rivers.

60 *Down with the New Tsars* (Peking, 1969), 19 (an official publication contain-ing Government statements and press articles).

61 By the Treaty of Nanking (1842), five ports including Canton and Shanghai were opened to British commerce, and Hong Kong was ceded to Britain.

62 Hertslet, *China Treaties* (1908), I 454.

63 Covering an area of about 60 × 30 km immediately south of what is now Blagoveshchensk.

64 The southern part of the Ussuri leading to the Korean frontier at a point about 13 miles from the Sea of Japan and 100 miles SW of Vladivostok. The demarcation was completed in 1861 with exchange of four maps.

65 About 150 miles south of Khabarovsk and the junction of the Amur and Ussuri rivers.

66 Kyakhta lies south of Lake Baikal and is now on the Russian side of the border. The Sayan range now forms the northern and eastern border of the Tuva ASSR.

67 MacMurray, *Treaties and Agreements with and covering China (1894–1911)* (1921), II 992, 1066.

68 Hertslet, op. cit., I 483.

69 A boundary agreement between Japan and Mongolia in June 1940, giving Mongolia some territory in Manchuria, of which Japan was then in occupation, was later renounced by China.

70 Hertslet, op. cit., I 462.

71 Issyk-Kul is a lake, about 30 miles south of Alma Ata and Ala Tau, a range of mountains, so there appears to be some confusion in at least the English text.

72 Kokand lies about 100 miles east of Tashkent.

73 See n. 68. The Treaty was drafted in three texts: Russian, Chinese and French.

74 For example, the oil and gas deposits recently found near Kashgar in north-western Xinjiang, which may be the same field as the important oil deposits around Alma Ata in the Kirghiz SSR.

75 See F. Parkinson, op. cit., Ch. 2.

76 For example, China-Japan Treaty (1978) Art. 2, described by Wolf Mendl in *World Today* (July 1979), 278.

77 Cited by M. Yahuda, *China's role in world affairs* (Croom Helm, 1978).

78 To be held one month after the signing of the agreement. The Conference achieved nothing under these Articles.

79 Garry L. Scott, *Chinese Treaties* (Oceana, 1975).

80 The International Court of Justice has not only not pronounced on the invalidity of 'unequal treaties', but appears to have accepted the inherent validity of at least capitulatory treaties in Morocco and Iran: see *Rights of US Nationals in Morocco* [1952], ICJ Reports 190, 200; *Anglo-Iranian Oil Co. Case (Jurisdiction)* [1952], ICJ Rep. 105, 106. Iran had in fact denounced all capitulatory treaties in 1927.

81 See generally A. L. W. Munkman, 'Adjudication and Adjustment: International Judicial Decision and the Settlement of Territorial and Boundary Disputes', 46 *BYIL* (1972–3), 1.

82 See Ian Brownlie, *African Boundaries* (C. Hurst, London; University of California Press, for RIIA, 1979), 10, 11.

83 (1933), RIAA, ii, 1322.

84 For compact factual surveys see M. J. Donelan and M. J. Grieve, *International Disputes: Case Histories 1945–1970* (Europa, 1973, for David Davies Memorial Institute). In particular, see the authoritative study of Cuba by Abram Chayes, *The Cuban Missile Crisis* (OUP, 1974); Robert R. Bowie, *Suez 1956* (OUP, 1974) and Coral Bell, *The Conventions of Crisis: A Study in Diplomatic Management* (OUP, 1971).

85 In a speech awarding the Louise Weiss Foundation Peace Prize to SIPRI (May 1979): *New Scientist* (12.7.1979), 129.

86 See Mohammed Ayoob, 'Superpowers and regional "stability" ', *World Today* (May 1979), 197.

87 Coral Bell, op. cit.

88 Krushchev is reported as admitting in March 1959 that the Western powers had 'lawful rights for their stay in Berlin': Donelan and Grieve, op. cit., 170.

89 Including a substantial number of medium-range and intermediate-range ballistic missiles and anti-aircraft missiles, with launchers; 42 medium-range jet bombers and 42 MIG-21 fighter aircraft; and over 20,000 troops to construct and operate the weapons system.

90 '. . . I, John F. Kennedy, President of the United States of America . . . do hereby proclaim that the forces under my command are ordered . . . to

interdict, subject to the instructions herein contained, the delivery of offensive weapons and associated material to Cuba': cited in Chayes, op. cit., 47.

91 Since such enforcement action must be different in character and scope from enforcement action by the Security Council, the observations of the ICJ on enforcement action in its advisory opinion on *Certain Expenses of the UN* [1962], ICJ Rep. 151, are not relevant.

92 Article 9: 'Ships owned or operated by a State and used only for government non-commercial service shall, on the high seas, have complete immunity from the jurisdiction of any State other than the flag State.'
Article 22 limits the boarding from a warship or a foreign merchant ship on the high seas to particular cases not arising in the quarantine, e.g. where the ship is engaged in piracy or the slave-trade.

93 The US had already used measures of economic coercion against the Castro régime: cancelling the Cuban sugar import quota in July 1960, and barring all exports to Cuba in October 1960, save of foodstuffs and medical supplies. The OAS adopted a resolution (16–1–4, including Brazil and Mexico) in January 1962 for suspension of trade in arms with Cuba.

94 The US response to Russian intervention in Afghanistan was similarly influenced.

95 On 2.8.1956: cited by Bowie, op. cit., 20.

96 Cited by Bowie, op. cit., 116.

97 *The Law of International Waterways* (Harvard UP, 1964), 52–71, where there is an excellent analysis and short history of the Company.

98 Statutes of the Company (1856), Articles 3, 24, 73, 74.

99 As the Egyptian Prize Court had held in the case of the *Flying Trader* [1950], *International Law Reports*, 440.

100 *The Economist* (22–8.3.1980), 47.

101 *United Nations Peacekeeping, 1946–1967*, I 62.

102 Resolution 3281–XXIX (December 1974): see Annex.

103 *Report of Bilateral Treaties for the Encouragement of International Private Investment* (ICC, November 1975), 9.

104 *17 International Legal Materials* (1978).

105 Reviewed by Malcolm Shaw in *International Relations* (November 1978), 415.

106 Given in the Report cited in n. 103, from which illustrative agreements are also quoted below.

107 See R. F. Mikesell, *Foreign Investment in Copper Mining* (1975), 26: 'An examination of existing mine development contracts of recent vintage reveals a bewildering combination of terms covering tax and royalty rates, tax holidays, depreciation schedules, loan-equity ratios, government and local public participation, government provision for infrastructure, import duties, land fees and rentals, and other conditions . . .'

108 R. E. Hudec, *The GATT Legal System and World Trade Diplomacy* (Praeger, 1975).

109 See Vincent Cable, 'Britain, the new protectionism and trade with the newly industrialising countries', *International Affairs* (January 1979), 1. The Generalized System of Preferences is itself circumscribed by import limits imposed on the processing of raw materials in the country of origin.

110 See the authoritative work of Rosalyn Higgins cited in n. 101.

111 By way of constitutional protection based on treaty provision: *Treaty of Berlin* (1878), Article V (freedom of religious belief and practice in Bulgaria); and of armed intervention in Greece leading to the *Treaty of Adrianople* (1827) accepted by Turkey which had maintained that 'l'affaire grecque est une affaire interne de la Sublime Porte.'

112 *in re Southern Rhodesia* [1919], AC 211 PC per Lord Sumner. For the evolution of Rhodesia see Claire Palley, *The Constitutional History and Law of Rhodesia, 1888–1965* (OUP, 1966). The principle that all 'acquisitions made under the influence of military force . . . do of right belong to the State' appears in a House of Commons Resolution in 1773, cited in Holdsworth, *History of English Law*, X 163.

113 Certain provisions were entrenched: the Declaration of Rights, drawn from the European Convention on Human Rights; Privy Council appeals; the Constitutional Council; the judiciary; and the power of amendment itself.

114 *Report of Central Africa Conference* (1963), § 21: *Cmnd 2093*.

115 Under the *Federation of Rhodesia and Nyasaland (Constitution) Order* (1953), Article 29: S.I. 1199/1953. Southern Rhodesia was an original Contracting Party to the GATT, but was an associate member of FAO (1959), ITU (1960) and the Economic Commission for Africa (1961). The Federation concluded trade and customs agreements with Israel and Portugal as well as with Commonwealth countries.

116 Calling for the release from detention of Joshua Nkomo and other nationalist leaders, and the lifting of the ban on the Zimbabwe African People's Union (ZAPU).

117 *Contemporary Survey* (1962–II), 250.

118 'Members of the United Nations which have or assume responsibilities for the administration of territories whose peoples have not attained a full measure of self-government recognize the principle that the interests of the inhabitants of these territories are paramount and accept as a sacred trust the obligation . . .

(a) to ensure, with due respect for the culture of the peoples concerned, their political, economic, social and educational advancement, their just treatment, and their protection against abuses;

(b) to develop self-government, to take due account of the political aspirations of the peoples, and to assist them in the progressive development of their free institutions . . .'

119 *Rhodesia: Documents relating to Proposals for a Settlement* (1966), *Cmnd 3171.*

120 Resolutions 1747–XVI (28.6.1962); 1755–XVII (31.10.1962) calling for suspension of the Constitution (1961); 1883–XVIII; 1889–XVIII (6.11.1963).

121 The constitutional establishment of Zimbabwe was finally achieved in 1980.

122 *20 UN Security Council Official Records 1258th Meeting* (1965), 21–2.

123 'The Security Council shall determine [*constate*] the existence of any threat to the peace, breach of the peace, or act of aggression, and shall make recommendations or decide [*décide*] what measures shall be taken in accordance with Articles 41 and 42, to maintain or restore international peace and security.'

124 The enlargement of the Security Council, from eleven to fifteen members, was initiated in 1963 and became effective in 1965, elections taking place in the autumn session of the General Assembly.

125 By 11 (Argentina, China, Japan, Jordan, Netherlands, New Zealand, Nigeria, Uganda, UK, USA, Uruguay)—0 with 4 abstentions (Bulgaria, France, Mali, USSR).

126 C. Lloyd Brown-John, *Multilateral Sanctions in International Law* (Praeger, 1975), Ch. 5.

127 Article 15(8).

128 'Nothing contained in the present Charter shall authorise the United Nations to intervene in matters which are essentially within the domestic jurisdiction of any State (*des affaires qui relèvent essentiellement de la*

compétence nationale d'un Etat) or shall require Members to submit such matters to settlement under the present Charter; but this principle shall not prejudice the application of enforcement measures under Chapter VII.'

129 Quoted in F. Parkinson, op. cit., n. 38.

130 From the joint blockade by Great Britain, France and Russia, of part of the Greek coast in 1827, to force Turkey to grant independence to Greece, there were at least twenty instances of pacific blockade by European powers.

131 UN Doc. S/5773.

132 Figures quoted by James Barber, 'Economic Sanctions as a Policy Instrument', *International Affairs* (July 1979), 367.

133 SCOR (October–December 1964), 186.

134 Principle VI states that: 'The participating States will refrain from any intervention, direct or indirect, *individual or collective*, in the internal affairs *falling within the domestic jurisdiction* of another participating State, regardless of their mutual relations' (italics added). The remainder of the Principle does not differ essentially from the UN Resolutions.

135 'All Members shall refrain in their international relations from the threat or use of force against the territorial integrity or political independence of any State, or in any other manner inconsistent with the Purposes of the United Nations.'

136 Addressing his Moscow constituents: *The Times* (23.2.1980).

137 Article 1 of the Charter declares that a purpose of the United Nations is: '(3) to achieve international cooperation in solving international problems of an economic, social, cultural or humanitarian character, and in promoting and encouraging respect for human rights and for fundamental freedoms for all without distinction as to race, sex, language, or religion.'

138 Quoted by I. Lapenna, 'Soviet concept of socialist international law', *29 YBWA* (1975), 242.

139 *The People's Daily* (1.11.1977) quoted in M. Yahuda, op. cit.

140 Article 1(1): 'All peoples have the right of self-determination. By virtue of that right they freely determine their political status and freely pursue their economic, social and cultural development.'

141 *Six Crises* (1968), 384, quoted by R. A. Falk, 'The Cambodian operation and international law', *69 AJIL* (1971), 1.

142 R. Fisher, *Points of Choice* (OUP, 1978), 34.

143 'The Realities of Detente', *International Herald Tribune* (13.1.1978).

Annex

CHARTER OF ECONOMIC RIGHTS
AND DUTIES OF STATES

Preamble

The General Assembly,

Reaffirming the fundamental purposes of the United Nations, in particular the maintenance of international peace and security, the development of friendly relations among nations and the achievement of international co-operation in solving international problems in the economic and social fields,

Affirming the need for strengthening international co-operation in these fields,

Reaffirming further the need for strengthening international co-operation for development,

Declaring that it is a fundamental purpose of the present Charter to promote the establishment of the new international economic order, based on equity, sovereign equality, interdependence, common interest and co-operation among all States, irrespective of their economic and social systems,

Desirous of contributing to the creation of conditions for:

(*a*) The attainment of wider prosperity among all countries and of higher standards of living for all peoples,

(*b*) The promotion by the entire international community of the economic and social progress of all countries, especially developing countries,

(*c*) The encouragement of co-operation, on the basis of mutual advantage and equitable benefits for all peace-loving States which are willing to carry out the provisions of the present Charter, in the economic, trade, scientific and technical fields, regardless of political, economic or social systems,

(*d*) The overcoming of main obstacles in the way of the economic development of the developing countries, (*e*) The acceleration of the economic growth of developing countries with a view to bridging the economic gap between developing and developed countries,

(*f*) The protection, preservation and enhancement of the environment,

Mindful of the need to establish and maintain a just and equitable economic and social order through:

(*a*) The achievement of more rational and equitable international economic relations and the encouragement of structural changes in the world economy,

(*b*) The creation of conditions which permit the further expansion of trade and intensification of economic co-operation among all nations,

(*c*) The strengthening of the economic independence of developing countries,

(*d*) The establishment and promotion of international economic relations, taking into account the agreed differences in development of the developing countries and their specific needs,

Determined to promote collective economic security for development, in particular of the developing countries, with strict respect for the sovereign equality of each State and through the co-operation of the entire international community,

Considering that genuine co-operation among States, based on joint consideration of and concerted action regarding international economic problems, is essential for fulfilling the international community's common desire to achieve a just and rational development of all parts of the world,

Stressing the importance of ensuring appropriate conditions for the conduct of normal economic relations among all States, irrespective of differences in social and economic systems, and for the full respect of the rights of all peoples, as well as strengthening instruments of international economic co-operation as a means for the consolidation of peace for the benefit of all,

Convinced of the need to develop a system of international economic relations on the basis of sovereign equality, mutual and equitable benefit and the close interrelationship of the interests of all States,

Reiterating that the responsibility for the development of every country rests primarily upon itself but that concomitant and effective international co-operation is an essential factor for the full achievement of its own development goals,

Firmly convinced of the urgent need to evolve a substantially improved system of international economic relations,

Solemnly adopts the present Charter of Economic Rights and Duties of States.

CHAPTER I

Fundamentals of international economic relations

Economic as well as political and other relations among States shall be governed, *inter alia*, by the following principles:

(a) Sovereignty, territorial integrity and political independence of States;

(b) Sovereign equality of all States;

(c) Non-aggression;

(d) Non-intervention;

(e) Mutual and equitable benefit;

(f) Peaceful coexistence;

(g) Equal rights and self-determination of peoples;

(h) Peaceful settlement of disputes;

(i) Remedying of injustices which have been brought about by force and which deprive a nation of the natural means necessary for its normal development;

(j) Fulfilment in good faith of international obligations;

(k) Respect for human rights and fundamental freedoms;

(l) No attempt to seek hegemony and spheres of influence;

(m) Promotion of international social justice;

(n) International co-operation for development;

(o) Free access to and from the sea by land-locked countries within the framework of the above principles.

CHAPTER II

Economic rights and duties of States

Article 1

Every State has the sovereign and inalienable right to choose its economic system as well as its political, social and cultural systems in accordance with the will of its people, without outside interference, coercion or threat in any form whatsoever.

129

Article 2

1. Every State has and shall freely exercise full permanent sovereignty, including possession, use and disposal, over all its wealth, natural resources and economic activities.

2. Each State has the right:

(*a*) To regulate and exercise authority over foreign investment within its national jurisdiction in accordance with its laws and regulations and in conformity with its national objectives and priorities. No State shall be compelled to grant preferential treatment to foreign investment;

(*b*) To regulate and supervise the activities of transnational corporations within its national jurisdiction and take measures to ensure that such activities comply with its laws, rules and regulations and conform with its economic and social policies. Transnational corporations shall not intervene in the internal affairs of a host State. Every State should, with full regard for its sovereign rights, co-operate with other States in the exercise of the right set forth in this subparagraph;

(*c*) To nationalize, expropriate or transfer ownership of foreign property, in which case appropriate compensation should be paid by the State adopting such measures, taking into account its relevant laws and regulations and all circumstances that the State considers pertinent. In any case where the question of compensation gives rise to a controversy, it shall be settled under the domestic law of the nationalizing State and by its tribunals, unless it is freely and mutually agreed by all States concerned that other peaceful means be sought on the basis of the sovereign equality of States and in accordance with the principle of free choice of means.

Article 3

In the exploitation of natural resources shared by two or more countries, each State must co-operate on the basis of a system of information and prior consultations in order to achieve optimum use of such resources without causing damage to the legitimate interest of others.

Article 4

Every State has the right to engage in international trade and other forms of economic co-operation irrespective of any differences in political, economic and social systems. No State shall be subjected to discrimination of any kind based solely on such differences. In the pursuit of international trade and other forms of economic co-operation, every State is free to choose the forms of organization of its foreign economic relations and to enter into bilateral and multilateral arrangements consistent with its international obligations and with the needs of international economic co-operation.

Article 5

All States have the right to associate in organizations of primary commodity producers in order to develop their national economies, to achieve stable financing for their development and, in pursuance of their aims, to assist in the promotion of sustained growth of the world economy, in particular accelerating the development of developing countries. Correspondingly, all States have the duty to respect that right by refraining from applying economic and political measures that would limit it.

Article 6

It is the duty of States to contribute to the development of international trade of goods, particularly by means of arrangements and by the conclusion of long-term multilateral commodity agreements, when appropriate, and taking into account the interests of producers and consumers. All States share the responsibility to promote the regular flow and access of all commercial goods traded at stable, remunerative and equitable prices, thus contributing to the equitable development of the world economy, taking into account, in particular, the interests of developing countries.

Article 7

Every State has the primary responsibility to promote the economic, social and cultural development of its people. To this end, each State has the right and the responsibility to choose its means and goals of development, fully to mobilize and use its resources, to implement progressive economic and social reforms and to ensure the full participation of its people in the process and benefits of development. All States have the duty, individually and collectively, to co-operate in eliminating obstacles that hinder such mobilization and use.

Article 8

States should co-operate in facilitating more rational and equitable international economic relations and in encouraging structural changes in the context of a balanced world economy in harmony with the needs and interests of all countries, especially developing countries, and should take appropriate measures to this end.

Article 9

All States have the responsibility to co-operate in the economic, social, cultural, scientific and technological fields for the promotion of economic and social progress throughout the world, especially that of the developing countries.

Article 10

All States are juridically equal and, as equal members of the international community, have the right to participate fully and effectively in the international decision-making process in the solution of world economic, financial and monetary problems, *inter alia*, through the appropriate international organizations in accordance with their existing and evolving rules, and to share equitably in the benefits resulting therefrom.

Article 11

All States should co-operate to strengthen and continuously improve the efficiency of international organizations in implementing measures to stimulate the general economic progress of all countries, particularly of developing countries, and therefore should co-operate to adapt them, when appropriate, to the changing needs of international economic co-operation.

Article 12

1. States have the right, in agreement with the parties concerned to participate in subregional, regional and interregional co-operation in the pursuit of their economic and social development. All States

engaged in such co-operation have the duty to ensure that the policies of those groupings to which they belong correspond to the provisions of the present Charter and are outward-looking, consistent with their international obligations and with the needs of international economic co-operation, and have full regard for the legitimate interests of third countries, especially developing countries.

2. In the case of groupings to which the States concerned have transferred or may transfer certain competences as regards matters that come within the scope of the present Charter, its provisions shall also apply to those groupings in regard to such matters, consistent with the responsibilities of such States as members of such groupings. Those States shall co-operate in the observance by the groupings of the provisions of this Charter.

Article 13

1. Every State has the right to benefit from the advances and developments in science and technology for the acceleration of its economic and social development.

2. All States should promote international scientific and technological co-operation and the transfer of technology, with proper regard for all legitimate interests including, *inter alia*, the rights and duties of holders, suppliers and recipients of technology. In particular, all States should facilitate the access of developing countries to the achievements of modern science and technology, the transfer of technology and the creation of indigenous technology for the benefit of the developing countries in forms and in accordance with procedures which are suited to their economies and their needs.

3. Accordingly, developed countries should co-operate with the developing countries in the establishment, strengthening and development of their scientific and technological infrastructures and their scientific research and technological activities so as to help to expand and transform the economics of developing countries.

4. All States should co-operate in research with a view to evolving further internationally accepted guidelines or regulations for the transfer of technology, taking fully into account the interests of developing countries.

Article 14

Every State has the duty to co-operate in promoting a steady and increasing expansion and liberalization of world trade and an improvement in the welfare and living standards of all peoples, in particular those of developing countries. Accordingly, all States should co-operate, *inter alia*, towards the progressive dismantling of obstacles to trade and the improvement of the international framework for the conduct of world trade and, to these ends, co-ordinated efforts shall be made to solve in an equitable way the trade problems of all countries, taking into account the specific trade problems of the developing countries. In this connexion, States shall take measures aimed at securing additional benefits for the international trade of developing countries so as to achieve a substantial increase in their foreign exchange earnings, the diversification of their exports, the acceleration of the rate of growth of their trade, taking into account their development needs, an improvement in the possibilities for these countries to participate in the expansion of world trade and a balance more favourable to developing countries in the sharing of the advantages resulting from this expansion, through, in the largest possible measure, a substantial improvement in the conditions of access for the products of interest to the developing countries and, wherever appropriate, measures designed to attain stable, equitable and remunerative prices for primary products.

Article 15

All States have the duty to promote the achievement of general and complete disarmament under effective international control and to utilize the resources released by effective disarmament measures for the economic and social development of countries, allocating a substantial portion of such resources as additional means for the development needs of developing countries.

Article 16

1. It is the right and duty of all States, individually and collectively, to eliminate colonialism, *apartheid*, racial discrimination, neo-colonialism and all forms of foreign aggression, occupation and domination, and the economic and social consequences thereof, as a prerequisite for development. States which practise such coercive policies are economically responsible to the countries, territories and peoples affected for the restitution and full compensation for the exploitation and depletion of, and damages to, the natural and all

other resources of those countries, territories and peoples. It is the duty of all States to extend assistance to them.

2. No State has the right to promote or encourage investments that may constitute an obstacle to the liberation of a territory occupied by force.

Article 17

International co-operation for development is the shared goal and common duty of all States. Every State should co-operate with the efforts of developing countries to accelerate their economic and social development by providing favourable external conditions and by extending active assistance to them, consistent with their development needs and objectives, with strict respect for the sovereign equality of States and free of any conditions derogating from their sovereignty.

Article 18

Developed countries should extend, improve and enlarge the system of generalized non-reciprocal and non-discriminatory tariff preferences to the developing countries consistent with the relevant agreed conclusions and relevant decisions as adopted on this subject, in the framework of the competent international organizations. Developed countries should also give serious consideration to the adoption of other differential measures, in areas where this is feasible and appropriate and in ways which will provide special and more favourable treatment, in order to meet the trade and development needs of the developing countries. In the conduct of international economic relations the developed countries should endeavour to avoid measures having a negative effect on the development of the national economies of the developing countries, as promoted by generalized tariff preferences and other generally agreed differential measures in their favour.

Article 19

With a view to accelerating the economic growth of developing countries and bridging the economic gap between developed and developing countries, developed countries should grant generalized preferential, non-reciprocal and non-discriminatory treatment to developing countries in those fields of international economic co-operation where it may be feasible.

Article 20

Developing countries should, in their efforts to increase their over-all trade, give due attention to the possibility of expanding their trade with socialist countries, by granting to these countries conditions for trade not inferior to those granted normally to the developed market economy countries.

Article 21

Developing countries should endeavour to promote the expansion of their mutual trade and to this end may, in accordance with the existing and evolving provisions and procedures of international agreements where applicable, grant trade preferences to other developing countries without being obliged to extend such preferences to developed countries, provided these arrangements do not constitute an impediment to general trade liberalization and expansion.

Article 22

1. All States should respond to the generally recognized or mutually agreed development needs and objectives of developing countries by promoting increased net flows of real resources to the developing countries from all sources, taking into account any obligations and commitments undertaken by the States concerned, in order to reinforce the efforts of developing countries to accelerate their economic and social development.

2. In this context, consistent with the aims and objectives mentioned above and taking into account any obligations and commitments undertaken in this regard, it should be their endeavour to increase the net amount of financial flows from official sources to developing countries and to improve the terms and conditions thereof.

3. The flow of development assistance resources should include economic and technical assistance.

Article 23

To enhance the effective mobilization of their own resources, the developing countries should strengthen their economic co-operation and expand their mutual trade so as to accelerate their economic and social development. All countries, especially developed countries, individually as well as through the competent international organizations of which they are members, should provide appropriate and effective support and co-operation.

Article 24

All States have the duty to conduct their mutual economic relations in a manner which takes into account the interests of other countries. In particular, all States should avoid prejudicing the interests of developing countries.

Article 25

In furtherance of world economic development, the international community, especially its developed members, shall pay special attention to the particular needs and problems of the least developed among the developing countries, of land-locked developing countries and also island developing countries, with a view to helping them to overcome their particular difficulties and thus contribute to their economic and social development.

Article 26

All States have the duty to coexist in tolerance and live together in peace, irrespective of differences in political, economic, social and cultural systems, and to facilitate trade between States having different economic and social systems. International trade should be conducted without prejudice to generalized non-discriminatory and non-reciprocal preferences in favour of developing countries, on the basis of mutual advantage, equitable benefits and the exchange of most-favoured-nation treatment.

Article 27

1. Every State has the right to enjoy fully the benefits of world invisible trade and to engage in the expansion of such trade.

2. World invisible trade, based on efficiency and mutual and equitable benefit, furthering the expansion of the world economy, is

the common goal of all States. The role of developing countries in world invisible trade should be enhanced and strengthened consistent with the above objectives, particular attention being paid to the special needs of developing countries.

Article 28

All States have the duty to co-operate in achieving adjustments in the prices of exports of developing countries in relation to prices of their imports so as to promote just and equitable terms of trade for them, in a manner which is remunerative for producers and equitable for producers and consumers.

CHAPTER III

Common responsibilities towards the international community

Article 29

The sea-bed and ocean floor and the subsoil thereof, beyond the limits of national jurisdiction, as well as the resources of the area, are the common heritage of mankind. On the basis of the principles adopted by the General Assembly in resolution 2749 (XXV) of 17 December 1970, all States shall ensure that the exploration of the area and exploitation of its resources are carried out exclusively for peaceful purposes and that the benefits derived therefrom are shared equitably by all States, taking into account the particular interests and needs of developing countries; an international régime applying to the area and its resources and including appropriate international machinery to give effect to its provisions shall be established by an international treaty of a universal character, generally agreed upon.

Article 30

The protection, preservation and enhancement of the environment for the present and future generations is the responsibility of all States. All States shall endeavour to establish their own environmental and developmental policies in conformity with such responsibility. The environmental policies of all States should enhance and not adversely affect the present and future development potential of developing countries. All States have the responsibility to ensure that activities within their jurisdiction or control do not cause damage to the environment of other States or of areas beyond the limits of national jurisdiction. All States should co-operate in evolving international norms and regulations in the field of the environment.

CHAPTER IV

Final provisions

Article 31

All States have the duty to contribute to the balanced expansion of the world economy, taking duly into account the close inter-relationship between the well-being of the developed countries and the growth and development of the developing countries, and the fact that the prosperity of the international community as a whole depends upon the prosperity of its constituent parts.

No State may use or encourage the use of economic, political or any other type of measures to coerce another State in order to obtain from it the subordination of the exercise of its sovereign rights.

Article 33

1. Nothing in the present Charter shall be construed as impairing or derogating from the provisions of the Charter of the United Nations or actions taken in pursuance thereof.

2. In their interpretation and application, the provisions of the present Charter are interrelated and each provision should be construed in the context of the other provisions.

Article 34

An item on the Charter of Economic Rights and Duties of States shall be included in the agenda of the General Assembly at its thirtieth session, and thereafter on the agenda of every fifth session. In this way a systematic and comprehensive consideration of the implementation of the Charter, covering both progress achieved and any improvements and additions which might become necessary, would be carried out and appropriate measures recommended. Such consideration should take into account the evolution of all the economic, social, legal and other factors related to the principles upon which the present Charter is based and on its purpose.

2315 plenary meeting
12 December 1974